Tony Baker

About the Author

ART BERG was the author of two regional bestsellers, *Some Miracles Take Time* and *Finding Peace in Troubled Waters*, and was the president of Invictus Communications, Inc. He spoke to hundreds of professional and civic organizations each year, including IBM, Sun Microsystems, AT&T, Coca-Cola, and Novell. He is survived by his wife and three children; they live in Highland, Utah.

The Impossible
Just Takes a Little
Longer

Quill
An Imprint of HarperCollinsPublishers

The Impossible

Just Takes a Little

Longer

LIVING WITH PURPOSE

AND PASSION

ART BERG

HarperCollins books may be purchased for educational, business,
or sales promotional use. For information please write:
Special Markets Department, HarperCollins Publishers Inc.,
10 East 53rd Street, New York, NY 10022.

First Quill edition published 2003.

Designed by Nicola Ferguson

The Library of Congress has catalogued the hardcover edition as follows:
Berg, Art E.
The impossible just takes a little longer :
living with purpose and passion / by Art Berg.
p.   cm.
ISBN 0-06-019990-3
1. Success. 2. Berg, Art E. I. Title.
BJ1611.2 .B45   2002
170'.44—dc21   2001044898

ISBN 0-06-051213-X (pbk.)

03 04 05 06 07 ❖/RRD 10 9 8 7 6 5 4 3 2 1

To my children, McKenzie and Dalton,
who live each day with purpose and passion

CONTENTS

PART FOUR: The Joy of the Journey

FOREWORD

TONY ROBBINS

For more than twenty years, I have been trying to help people understand how they can stretch beyond themselves and unleash a magnificent power that lies within. Art Berg embodies that magnificent power.

Art has endured the kind of trials and struggles that few of us can even imagine. Yet he simply has refused to put limits on his life. He has defied the odds, defied the naysayers, defied the cultural hypnosis that says so many things cannot be done, and has driven himself to amazing levels of personal achievement and accomplishment. He has refused to let go of his own inner hunger for excellence, that overwhelming imperative to live in a way that will never let him settle for anything less than he is capable of being.

We all have that inner hunger. It is what I like to call our "driving force." And if there is one thing I have learned through counseling some of the world's most well-known leaders, as well as in dealing with drug addicts and the clinically depressed, it is that there is only one way to obtain real fulfillment and make a significant difference in your life and in the lives of those around you: You, too, must tap into that deep inner hunger, that emotional state of defiance, that tenacious determination to create opportunities for yourself and create an extraordinary life.

Art Berg will inspire you to reignite your own driving force. I have never met anyone else who has had a greater impact on people's lives through the sheer force of his own life's experience. I see him do it every year when he comes to speak at my annual nine-day Mastery University in Hawaii. Here is a man, the audiences realize, who does not let fear control him, who does not recognize the term "failure," who believes life is not worth living unless you are living up to your full potential.

For those of you who have lost your way or who are scared of facing change, Art Berg is the man for you. He is truly an amazing example of human potential—a living treasure.

The foreword above was written in late 2001. In February 2002, my friend Art Berg died in his sleep. His death was sudden, and left all of us who loved and admired him reeling with shock and sadness.

In my original foreword, I refer to Art as a "living treasure." I stand by that statement, even today, more than a year after his death. For, Art is alive in the pages of this book; his message of courage and conviction, purpose and passion, is as vital, illuminating, and important today as it ever was. As Art would say, if he were here: *Invictus!*

PREFACE

A TRAGEDY? OR A BLESSING?

I'm about to tell you a story. It is a story that you will no doubt call a tragedy. You will say to yourself that life should not be so unfair, so cruel, so painful. You will call me an innocent victim of fate. You will insist that no one, especially someone trying to live a good life, should have had to suffer the way I did.

But before you finish this book, I want you to ask yourself a few questions: Did I really endure a tragedy, or was I given one of the most significant opportunities of my life? Did my life turn into a disaster, or had I been given one of the most significant blessings that I will ever enjoy?

Had I, in fact, been given a rare chance to learn what it

really means to discover the best part of myself? To live a life full of meaning, a life that actually allowed me to control my own destiny, regardless of what had happened to me in the past and regardless of what would happen to me in the future?

That is what this story is all about.

ACKNOWLEDGMENTS

T he *Impossible Just Takes a Little Longer* is not a story about me
as much as it is the collective efforts of many friends, family,
and associates over the years.

It was an enormous financial and emotional risk for me when I
began a career as a professional speaker. Others believed in me and
encouraged me when the growth curve seemed never-ending. Some
of my most ardent supporters and mentors included Dave Gorden,
Keith Harrell, Joel and Judy Weldon, Nido Qubein, Gil and Esther
Eagles, Tony Robbins, Jim and Naomi Rhode, Brian Holloway,
Rosita Perez, the Speakers Roundtable, Al Walker, Robert Henry,
Don Clark, and the National Speakers Association. There were also
bureaus that believed in me early on such as Keynote Speakers,

International Speakers Bureau, Leading Authorities, National Speakers Bureau, and Five Star Speakers & Trainers.

Friends and family have proved themselves invaluable when it has come to their constant faith in me. They have always challenged me to reach higher and to live with passion. These include many of our friends with whom we live and interact in Highland, Utah. In addition, from time to time a client becomes an enduring friend and supporter, such as David Modell, Brian Billick, Jeff Nugent, Peter Whitehead, Fernando Aguirre, Judy Marz, Bruce Nelson, and Dave Reed.

The impossible was made more probable by the encouragement and faith of my wife, Dallas, parents, siblings and extended family. During my darkest hours they never left my side.

Finally, it was the vision and efforts of my publisher, William Morrow, and editors Janet Dery, Diane Reverand, and Jennifer Brehl that have brought this book to your shelf. It all started as an idea that was made possible by the enthusiasm of Jan Miller and the loyalty of Dawnie Campagna.

INTRODUCTION: THE MAN WHO TAUGHT US "INVICTUS"

✺

Brian Billick

Coach of the Super Bowl XXXV Champion

Baltimore Ravens

In the muggy, heat-drenched summer of 2000, the football team that I coached, the NFL's Baltimore Ravens, gathered for its annual preseason football camp. We were then a team unsure of where we were going—a team uncertain of our destiny. The season before, we had produced an 8–8 record, which was not good enough to make the playoffs, and a lot of people were predicting we wouldn't get much better.

For one thing, our detractors said, two other teams in our division, the Tennessee Titans and the Jacksonville Jaguars, had put together two of the best win-loss records of any NFL team during the 1999 season, and the Titans had gone all the way to the Super Bowl. Both of those teams were coming back as strong and confident as ever.

Although we had a solid second half in the 1999 season, winning five of our last seven games, and although we had bolstered our team with an excellent group of free agents, we were searching for that level of confidence that would make us champions.

What's more, we faced a variety of off-the-field distractions. The media had descended on our training camp to hound our star defensive player, linebacker Ray Lewis, who had been arrested in the offseason on murder charges. Although the charges had been dropped and Lewis absolved of any responsibility for the crime, reporters were more than happy to keep the story on the front pages and add an atmosphere of controversy to what I had hoped would be a focused few weeks of practice.

Despite everything, I was still convinced that we could make the playoffs, and I said as much to the media. But I knew that if we were to get there, my players needed to absolutely believe that this was their year. They needed to develop a vision about what they could accomplish. And they needed to learn how to maintain that vision regardless of what happened during the season.

No group of players reaches the championship game without overcoming significant adversity, whether it be injuries, frustration, offensive slumps, hostile crowds on the road, or even bad calls from the officials. I wanted my players to know that their challenge lay not in avoiding adversity, but in overcoming it. I wanted them to understand what could happen to us as a team if each of them did just one little thing to improve their individual performance, if they found one way to step up their commitment and discipline.

And I knew exactly the person to give my players that message. One morning after breakfast, I called a team meeting at the hotel where we were staying. The players sat down, and I said, "Gentlemen, before you go out to practice, I want you to listen to somebody." Then Art Berg rolled out onto a little makeshift stage in his wheelchair.

Needless to say, it was an intriguing moment: A man who for seventeen years hadn't been able to walk or even stand was about to speak to a group of burly, muscular players who were in nearly perfect physical shape. These were guys who had been hearing rah-rah speeches since their very first Pee Wee league football practices. They had been listening to inspirational slogans from coaches like me for so long that they could probably repeat them by memory.

Just a few feet away from Art on the stage were the great tight end Shannon Sharpe, the highly touted rookie running back Jamal Lewis, quarterback Trent Dilfer, and, of course, the fierce, intimidating, no-nonsense members of the Ravens' defensive squad.

Yet this man, sitting quietly in his wheelchair, unable to move most of his body, was about to touch something deep inside them in a way they had never been touched before.

If you do not yet know Art Berg, I am proud to introduce him. He is one of the most popular motivational speakers in America, who travels more than 200,000 miles a year telling people about the power of the human spirit. He unabashedly tells audiences what happened to him in the middle of the night on a Nevada highway—a story that you will soon read for yourself in these pages. He talks about how he found himself at a place in life where it seemed as if he had no control whatsoever over his destiny. Yet he then tells you how he remembered, even in the midst of an unspeakable tragedy, that he alone, and no one else, could determine the meaning of his life. And what happened next, as you will soon find out, is a remarkable story of perseverance, dedication, and triumph.

When Art told his story to the Ravens, I thought the room was going to explode. You could see the passion in the players' eyes as they leaped to their feet and gave him a standing ovation. On that morning, Art taught us all about our sense of destiny. He taught us all that controlling our destiny doesn't mean controlling the events that happen in our lives. It means choosing how we respond to those events. Controlling one's destiny doesn't mean focusing on what you don't have. It means focusing on what to do with what you do have.

At the end of his speech, he told us about a young nineteenth-century Englishman named William Ernest Henley, who had been struck down in the prime of his life with a crippling disease. Left in a hospital and expected to die within weeks, he wrote a now-famous poem, which he titled "Invictus":

> Out of the night that covers me,
> Black as the Pit from pole to pole,
> I thank whatever gods may be,
> For my unconquerable soul.
>
> In the fell clutch of circumstance,
> I have not winced nor cried aloud;
> Under the bludgeonings of chance
> My head is bloody, but unbowed.
>
> Beyond this place of wrath and tears
> Looms but the Horror of the shade,
> And yet the menace of the years
> Finds, and shall find me, unafraid.
>
> It matters not how strait the gate,
> How charged with punishments the scroll,
> I am the master of my fate;
> I am the captain of my soul.

"*Invictus*," Art told us, is a Latin word that means "unconquered, unsubdued, invincible." As it turned out, the word perfectly fit

William Ernest Henley. The doctors had been forced to amputate one leg just below the knee, and they told him days later that if he wanted to live, they would need to amputate the other leg.

No, said Henley. He was going to survive without that second operation, he proclaimed. And after eighteen long months, he did indeed walk away from that hospital, never to return.

The story was so moving that we had copies of the poem laminated and given to each player, and by the time the season began, the word *"invictus"* had become our rallying cry. After each home game victory, the team's president, the son of the Ravens' owner, had *"Invictus"* flashed up on our scoreboard. It was our way of saying that we knew we were certain of our destiny, certain that we could rise above any adversity.

We did make the playoffs. We went all the way to the Super Bowl. Our defense, led by MVP Ray Lewis, turned out to be arguably the best in the history of professional football. And just before that game, at a team meeting in the locker room, I reminded the players about that long-ago day the previous summer when Art Berg came to our training camp to tell us his story. "Today," I said, "we will play with the invictus attitude. We will walk off that field unconquered, unsubdued, invincible."

And we did. The Ravens put on one of the most dominant performances in Super Bowl history, beating the New York Giants 34–7.

I will never forget Art Berg. He was a unique catalyst for me and my team, an inspiration who helped us reach a place in that championship season that no one believed we could get to. For that reason, we awarded Art his own Super Bowl ring, the word "Invictus" inscribed on its side. You will never forget him, either. *The Impossible Just Takes a Little Longer* is a rare book that contains both gentle compassion and brutal honesty, graceful wisdom and practical insight. Art's message is not just for those who face particular tragedies and suffering of their own. It is also for those who are still searching for their own sense of destiny, who want to know that their lives really matter, who want to know that they, too, can rise up despite all the pain, the disappointment, and the frustration that they have encountered.

This is not an abstract book. Art does not try to use big words or clever ways of rephrasing questions in an effort to convince you that your problems are not really problems. Actually, he does just the opposite. As you read his stories about his own life—from the moment he realized he could not feel his legs, to his attempts just to relearn how to hold a pen, to his staggering accomplishment when he set a world record racing in a 325-mile ultra-marathon in his wheelchair—you will realize what amazing personal power you can find simply through the process of meeting and solving your problems.

You will find some of his stories immensely funny—like the one he tells of his attempt to learn to scuba dive despite being a quadriplegic—and you'll find others tearfully poignant. But, most of all, you'll find a great sense of hope in *The Impossible Just Takes a Little Longer*. You'll realize that this is your chance to finally move away from the pack of those who just talk about doing something with their lives. This is your moment to create a life of deep significance and true satisfaction. This is your time to live with the invictus attitude.

PART ONE

When Life Has
You Paralyzed

ONE

Finding the Courage to Transform Your Life

It was Christmas 1983, and I was happier than I had ever been in my life. I had just started my own company and I was engaged to the most beautiful girl in the world. I was in top physical shape, a competitive water-skier and snow skier. I played golf, tennis, racquetball, and basketball. I was a competitive bowler, and I ran several miles every day.

It was a time in my life when it was hard to imagine anything tripping me up. I was young, articulate, confident, and ambitious. I believed God had great plans for my future.

I celebrated Christmas Day with my parents and brothers and sisters at our home in San Jose, California, and then I prepared to leave that evening for Utah to spend the rest of the holidays with my fiancée, Dallas, where we would finish preparing for our wedding, which would take place in five weeks. I had made the California-to-Utah trip dozens of times through the years with friends and family. It was hardly a big deal. On that Christmas Day, I had a prayer with my family before I left, praying for the usual things. We asked God to watch over me and to provide me with a safe journey.

At about 7:00 in the evening, I said goodbye to my family, and got into a little car with a new friend of mine named John. We had decided to drive the southern route through Nevada in order to avoid any possibility of snow over the northern mountain passes of California. I took the wheel first. I was excited. In fifteen short hours, I'd be with my future bride. Dallas and I had met when we were teenagers and we knew almost from the day we laid eyes on one another that we were meant to be together.

After eight hours of driving, my eyes felt heavy and John took over. I climbed into the passenger's seat, fastened my seat belt, and went to sleep while my friend drove in the darkness.

An hour and a half later, I was suddenly awakened as I felt the car swerve. We were forty miles north of Las Vegas on Interstate 15. John had fallen asleep at the wheel, lost control of the car, a little Volkswagen Rabbit, and was heading for a cement barrier along the right side of the highway. The tires rode the embankment to the top of the barrier, hurtled into the air, then the car flipped several times as it rolled off the side of the road.

The car finally came to a stop in a pile of twisted metal and broken glass. John quickly turned to his right to see if I was okay, but I wasn't there. Quickly he pulled himself through a broken window and called my name.

He heard only the quiet sounds of a gentle wind whispering back. "Art!" he yelled again, running blindly in the darkness, stumbling over the rough terrain.

No answer.

Finally, on hands and knees, John groped through the thick

darkness, feeling his way, calling my name again and again. After what seemed an eternity, he heard soft groans.

I was laying on the desert floor. Blood was streaming down my face. John pulled his leather jacket from off his shoulders, spread it across my broken body, and then asked, "Are you all right?"

I told him I didn't think so. I told him I couldn't move my legs, that I couldn't feel my hands.

"God, please help me," I whispered, and then I slipped into unconsciousness.

It took more than an hour for an ambulance to arrive. I was raced to Las Vegas Valley Hospital, and during the entire trip, my friend John and the ambulance attendant tried to keep me awake, aware that I was in danger of shutting my eyes for the last time.

"What day is it?" asked the attendant.

I didn't know.

"What day was yesterday?" he asked.

I still didn't know.

"It was a special day, a holiday day, do you remember?"

I searched my mind. Nothing.

He tried again. "How many lights do you see on the ceiling?"

I responded, "Four." At least I was making some progress.

"Who were you going to see in Utah?" was the last question I remember being asked.

"My sweetheart—the most beautiful girl in the world," I said. Later, the ambulance attendant and John told me I was smiling. The smile softened my mouth, then I slipped once more into unconsciousness.

I would not smile again for a long time. After I arrived at the hospital, I was taken straight into an operating room, where I underwent four hours of surgery to try to mend my neck. It had been broken at the fifth vertebra from the top. If the break had been a little higher, I would have most assuredly been dead. Doctors made an incision about three inches long on the front of my neck to fuse the three vertebrae together. A tube was connected to the back of my neck to help drain off the excess blood. In an effort to keep me nourished, other tubes had been pushed through my nose into my stomach. Cold metal tongs of traction were bolted into the sides of my head, with thirty pounds of weight to keep the pressure off the wounded area. The sides of my head had been shaved to provide a clean surface for the tongs to be inserted.

When I finally awakened, a doctor leaned down and said to me, as gently as he could, "Art, you are a quadriplegic." I had lost the use of my feet and legs. I had lost the use of all my stomach muscles and two of three major chest muscles. I had lost the use of my right triceps. I had lost most of the use of my shoulders and arms. And I had lost all use of my hands.

The doctor calmly laid out the facts. He said I would always need someone to help me get dressed, to help me eat, and to help me move from place to place. I would never drive. I would never work again, because 93 percent of the people in my condition never did. I would never be able to play any kind of sports. I was told that I would likely never get married or have children. I was given a list of prescription drugs that the doctor said I would need to take for the rest of my life. But even then, the doctor said, I would probably die prematurely.

"For the rest of the life you have left," said that doctor said as he stood over my bed, "you're going to have to dream new dreams, think new thoughts."

Let me take a wild guess at what you're thinking. You are probably sitting in a comfortable chair, reading right along, and you're saying to yourself, "Okay, this is a sad story and everything, but really, what does this have to do with me improving my life? What am I really going to learn by reading a story about some guy being in a bad car wreck?"

Whenever I give a speech, which I now do more than 150 times a year, I can sense that very reaction in the audience. They see me rolling out on stage, and they inwardly groan, wondering what they're in for. Some of them actually think I'm there as part of some plot by their bosses. I have been hired, they think, to give them a hard-luck, woe-is-me talk to make them feel guilty about how good they have it so that they will stop feeling sorry for themselves about how hard they have to work for their companies. "'Sure, I could be more appreciative of my life," they are thinking, "but I don't need to hear a speech about it. At the moment, I've got some problems of my own. I have some things going on in my own life—some disappointments, some frustration, some fear— that might not exactly be the same as a car wreck, but they are tough all the same."

To which I think, "Perfect. This is exactly the audience I'm trying to reach."

In fact, early on in my speeches I tell my audiences, "I know a lot of you are in pain, and I want you to know, it's no different than mine."

I can sense the silence beginning to sweep over the room. People start looking at me curiously, especially when I tell them that I know we have a lot in common. "Every one of you has your own set of fears, your own worries, your own obstacles—your own pain," I say. "And if I have learned anything other the years, it is that pain hurts in any form."

I tell them that the pain from my car wreck is no greater than the pain of a father financially struggling just to get food on the table for his children. I tell them that my tears are no wetter than the tears of a manager who just lost his job of twenty years. I tell them that my heart isn't any more broken than that of the parent who has lost his or her child to the influence of alcohol and drugs.

"I may be paralyzed physically," I say, "but I believe there are those of you here in this room today who may feel paralyzed, too. When you feel overwhelmed emotionally, spiritually, intellectually, or financially, when you're filled with a sense of uncertainty and doubt, unsure of the direction you should take, when your challenges seem bigger than your opportunities, then you can find yourself paralyzed—and it's a paralysis that can be just as devastating as the physical paralysis was for me."

In speech after speech, I look out at audiences—and my audiences range from teenagers to Fortune 500 sales teams, from hog farmers to the manufacturers of ladies' underwear, from top professional athletes to multimillionaires to stay-at-home mothers—and I can see that what I am saying is hitting home. I know that whenever I speak, there are some who are listening who face particular tragedies and suffering of their own, who feel beaten down by fate, who simply have lost their way. They might have done many good things in life, made many admirable accomplishments, and yet they still feel moments of the deepest dissatisfaction.

They feel stuck in their own private no-man's-land, not sure exactly what went wrong and not certain at all of what is required to take conscious control again of their lives. They might have become very successful financially, believing that certain possessions would let them create a "quality" life. But then they inevitably learn that their definition of "quality" never lasts, that financial success without fulfillment means nothing. They realize that what they want to achieve is not necessarily what they need to achieve.

Do you know what I'm talking about? Have you, too, ever felt that paralysis—one that makes you tentative and afraid, one that makes you doubt that the dreams you once had for yourself were going to come true? Have you ever endured the kinds of experiences that separated you from those dreams?

For a moment, I want you to consider your own life. I want you to ask yourself if you are living with purpose and passion, or are you languishing, living out a life of quiet (or perhaps very unquiet) desperation, unsure how to make the changes that you know, deep down, you must make to give your life greater significance?

Ask yourself: don't you want to know how to live so that your life matters, so that the world will have been far better for your having passed through it?

For the last two decades, I have been obsessed with that question. I have devoted my career to understanding what one must do to overcome disappointment and setbacks in order to find an extraordinary quality of life. When I travel the country giving speeches, or when I personally consult with thousands of people over the telephone or via e-mail, I spend almost all my time discussing the subject of how we face change, how we adapt to change, and how we must change ourselves to achieve a memorable, fulfilling life. What causes certain people to joyously live their lives out loud while others remain stuck in baffled or angry silence? Why are there people who have no family support, no education, no powerful background—yet who produce results far beyond anyone's expectations? And why are there people with superior education and superior talent who can't find the fulfillment they thought would be so simple to obtain?

No matter where I am or what I am doing, I have never stopped asking these questions. Why are there people who never stop searching desperately for a future, while there are others who go out and make their futures happen? Why are some propelled forward while others stay where they are? Why do some make great dents in the world, while others lose touch with their own passion?

I know there is an entire industry in this country that makes money trying to tell you the answers to those questions. We've got hordes of psychologists, psychiatrists, therapists, and emotional healers, all providing guidelines that are supposed to tell you the important "how-to's"—how to be creative, how to be intimate, how to feel happy. The only problem is, it doesn't seem to be working. People are still on a futile hunt to find the answers to end the stultifying emptiness of their lives.

Or if they aren't on that hunt, they are on an equally intense attempt to rationalize away their lives, telling themselves that at least they are secure and comfortable. They try to believe that it's okay to forget some of your dreams. They find themselves trying to stay closer to shore, refusing to venture out into the seas, refusing even to rock their own boat. They engage in fuzzy thinking, telling themselves that they know they "should" do something about their plight and that they know they "should" do something to make themselves feel better.

They say to themselves, over and over, that they'd like to change . . . but then they admit that they just aren't sure what to change into. Eventually, they start blaming circumstances for their place in life rather than making the effort to find the circumstances they want. They surround themselves with friends whose aspirations are even lower than their own.

In essence, they are stuck. They are paralyzed. Instead of feeling the exhilaration of life's possibilities, they feel compressed by life's narrowness. Their enthusiasm for change ebbs like the tide. Occasionally, they might try some psychological Band-Aid—a visit to a therapist, a self-help book, a motivational tape to listen to in the car. Or they might turn to any number of sedatives to deaden their gnawing hunger of dissatisfaction. They reach for some food, for example, briefly believing that they can get away with being full instead of being fulfilled. Some of them turn to alcohol or some other drug, briefly believing that a temporary change in their biochemistry will cause some change in the way they live. Or they will distract themselves with television or with parties or with even more overtime at the office.

But sooner or later, they have to come face-to-face with a very urgent question that must be answered: Is this really the way they want to live?

What I have learned—and what I want to pass on to you in this book—is that there is one, and only one, difference between those who live ordinary lives and those who rise above their circumstances to create something far more rewarding for themselves. It's not that these people have superior, God-given talent or greater willpower than you do. It's not that they have a ten-point program on how to be great that no one else knows about. It's not that they have a professional background in counseling or a doctorate in the helping professions.

What they have discovered is that they alone are responsible for giving their lives significance and satisfaction.

They have learned that there is no magic formula. The best way for them to work some magic in their lives is simply by believing the phrase, "I am responsible." They know that when it comes to creating happiness and instilling passion into one's life, they alone must do it. And here's the key: they must do it no matter what has happened to them and no matter what pain comes their way.

That's what this book is all about. It is about you living each moment for everything it's worth, regardless of what storms rage around you. This is a book to help you live that kind of life despite the struggles and the changes that you will constantly face. This is a book that will help you achieve a vision for yourself that will not be affected by any adversity that comes your way.

Are you thinking that this is silly self-help talk designed to sell a few books? Trust me, you can make gigantic changes in the way you live your life. You can indeed turn your back on a mediocre, secondhand existence, and you can discover a new kind of courage. You can learn to believe, not doubt. You can create, not follow. You can ignite in yourself that overwhelming imperative to succeed—to live in a state that never lets you settle for anything less than you are capable of being.

And the reason I am so convinced you can do it is because I did it. Even today, it is difficult for me to describe to you the shroud of despair that descended upon me as I lay on that desert floor. I cannot tell you what it felt like when those doctors told me after my long surgery that I was a quadriplegic. The statement slammed into my consciousness like a bullet. How could this be happening to me? I kept saying to myself that I had been a good person. I had tried to do what was right in the sight of God. This, however, did not make sense. This was not how the world was supposed to work. Tragedies were supposed to happen to selfish, dishonest people whom I, as a religious person, would then try to comfort by assuring them of God's forgiving love. They weren't supposed to happen to me. I was someone who had spent my youth dreaming of romance, adventure, success, and prosperity. I dreamed of beautiful sunsets, white horses, and living "happily ever after." Nowhere in those dreams was there a place for suffering. Nowhere in those dreams was there a scenario in which I would be the one who was afflicted.

I felt abandoned, left to fend for myself in a hospital room. I was so devastated, caught so completely off guard, I wondered how I ever would be able to survive. How, I asked myself, was I ever again to find happiness? How would I ever again feel delight? How would I ever again know what it means to be content? How was I ever going to have a life that mattered?

Then, not many hours after my surgery, I heard the voice of my mother, who had come to the hospital from California and had taken a seat at my bedside. "Art," she said, "while the difficult takes time, the impossible just takes a little longer."

There was a long silence. I gave her a look. My eyes filled with tears.

And then she whispered to me again, "Art, the impossible just takes a little longer."

PART TWO

Preparing for Your Journey to the Impossible

Four Questions to Ask About Your Life Today

TWO

Have You Ever Been Afraid?

For days after my accident, I could not sleep. Even though my body was exhausted from the trauma of the long surgery, I never drifted off for too long, for as soon as I did, I began to hear the very strange sound of laughter. It was hideous, diabolical laughter. It seemed to be coming from a hundred people. Then, after a few minutes, I would hear a voice cutting through the laughter.

At first, I couldn't understand what the voice was saying. But it gradually became louder. "I've got you now," the voice said. "I have destroyed your life. Without your body you are nothing. You will be miserable, you will be weak. And when your life is over, I will have won." Then, once again, the laughter returned—chilling laughter, haunted house–like laughter, waves and waves of laughter.

Terrified, I would try to lunge out of my hospital bed. I would focus all my energy on shifting my weight, just wiggling my toes—but there would be no movement whatsoever. The metal tongs that had been drilled into my skull kept me from moving my head. I could barely even glance to the left or the right. My body felt as though it weighed a hundred tons and I was trapped inside like a wounded, caged bird.

I kept wanting to scream. I would shut my eyes tightly and then open them, thinking that when I did, the nightmare would be over, that I would be back in California or in Utah with my fiancée. But the scene was always the same. There I was, in my frozen, motionless world, my limbs seemingly detached from the rest of me. Clusters of people in surgical uniforms came and went at all hours of the day and night. They checked the IV stuck in my arm and the catheter stuck in my bladder. They arranged and rearranged the equipment and supplies at my bedside table, the bottles, the gauze, the bandages, the scissors, the scalpels, the jars. I felt like a clinical case study, a repository for tubes and tongs. The light always seemed harsh, the sounds noisy and impersonal, the walls bare. There was the constant smell of antiseptic. My mouth felt like cotton, and it was hard to swallow.

Most of all, I felt a fear that I had never before known—a naked, animal-like fear that nauseated me. It was a fear so strong that I could almost smell it. Despite my despair that God had let this happen, I spent hours desperately praying to Him, asking that I be healed, promising Him anything if He would just let me avoid this pain. When there was no immediate answer, the fear only increased.

For hours, I would just lay there, staring at the ceiling. And when I would feel myself falling asleep, the laughter would return once more.

———

It is not likely, of course, that you are going to end up on a desert floor like I did and then be taken to a hospital where you will be told you are a quadriplegic. But let's get one thing straight right now. You will endure—if you have not endured it already—what St. John of the Cross once called "the dark night of the soul." You might not endure the same kind of physical affliction that I did, but you will endure affliction, whatever it may be. You will face agony. You will ask the same emotional, philosophical, and spiritual questions as I did in that hospital room. And you, too, will experience raw, unbridled fear.

I want you to think about what I just said. I mean, really think about it. All the time, I come across people who still define happiness as a life without pain, a life without too many problems, at least not big ones. They believe that fulfillment means (1) finding pleasure and (2) avoiding pain. For them, these are the twin forces that drive their behavior. That is their idea of "self-improvement."

Unfortunately, they are destined for the deepest unhappiness. They do not understand that there is no such thing as a smooth ride in life. They do not understand that life always involves struggle—and that they will not get a free pass from the pain.

The absolute reality is that when it comes to living, there are a thousand bumps along the way, some of them small, some of them jarring. With life comes illness and injury, rejection and disappointment, frustration and misfortune. You will endure unexpected turns and hardships, some that will blindside you by chance, and some that will be of your own making. You'll endure negative circumstances beyond your control, and you'll have to endure the consequences of your or someone else's poor decisions and self-destructive behaviors. Make no mistake: you will endure suffering—either the immense suffering that comes from a cataclysmic event like cancer, or the private suffering, which can be just as intense, that comes from a life of withdrawal, depression, betrayal, rejection, clawing competitiveness, bitter frustration, bafflement, compromise, or anger.

And if you think you can hide from life's problems—if you think you can find some Norman Rockwell–like environment that will bring you peace—think again. There is no more such town. Our problems are innumerable and endless, and they only seem to be increasing. I once read a report from the World Future Society that listed "2,653 problems facing humanity," a list ranging from nuclear war to plagues to financial concerns. We are a country in which 15 million people have been diagnosed as being clinically depressed. Although we make up just 5 percent of the world's population, we ingest 50 percent of the world's cocaine. Violent crime is rampant on the streets and at home. Suicide is increasing at an exponential rate. The institution of marriage continues to crumble. The divorce rate is estimated to be as high as 60 percent, and the average length of new marriages is now about 22 months. A woman born after 1960 is likely to have more husbands than children. (Yes, yes, I know there's probably a woman out there smirking and saying, "So what? There's no difference between the two.") And the sad truth is that the children we do have are not being all that well treated. The reported emotional neglect of children has increased 330 percent in the last decade. More than 45 percent of them experiment with alcohol by the time they reach the eighth grade, 25 percent with drugs.

We live in the fastest paced, most rapidly changing society in the history of humankind. Indeed, the changes are coming so fast that it is difficult to gain our footing, let alone predict the future. Not too many generations ago, we planned on going to work for the same company all our lives. Today, it is not uncommon for people to have not just four different jobs in a lifetime, but four different careers! The change is so dizzying that organizations are being asked to do in a year what used to take a decade. Just when you thought we were in the midst of an unparalleled economic boom, we now face a global recession and a shrinking job market. The ever-changing demands of a technological society have made holding a steady job as difficult as tap-dancing on quicksand. Unemployment rolls are swelling. Stock options are gone. People who bought beautiful homes a few years ago are now talking to bankruptcy attorneys.

In other words, the "good life" is not going to just happen to you. To grab ahold of the good life, then you must be prepared for the struggles that lay ahead—for the turmoil and the problems, for the pain that will cut through your heart and soul and perhaps even your body like a knife. You must be prepared for what the great psychiatrist Carl Jung referred to as "the night sea journey." It is that period in life when one feels lost in the wilderness, disconnected from all others, alienated and isolated from the very things that makes life seem worth living.

I know this is a concept that you've heard a half million times. But this time, as you begin your own journey to the impossible, I want to present to you an idea that could be a major pivot point in your life. The idea is going to sound so inherently contradictory that you initially might have trouble believing it. It certainly took me a long time to understand it. But here goes:

It is not a tragedy that life is a struggle. It is a blessing.

Once again, let me stop and try to guess what's rattling around in your brain. "A struggle is a blessing?" you're saying to yourself. "Isn't that just a little too pat of a line? Come on."

What if I also told you that those very struggles were actually going to be your best opportunities to develop the richer and more satisfying life you've always wanted?

And what if I told you that the key to your happiness is not to avoid life's struggles, but to go out of your way to deal with them?

In a famous short story, "The Death of Ivan Ilyich," Leo Tolstoy creates a character who seems successful—he has a good job and a nice family—but he has spent his entire life living tentatively, trying to avoid life's complications, problems, and pain. It is only at the end of his life that he realizes that he has never come close to the dreams that were once so important to him. Ivan Ilyich realizes that he has embraced nothing, faced no challenges, showed no passion, found no meaning. He realizes "that his professional duties and the whole arrangement of his life and of his family, and all his social and official interests, might all have been false. He tried to defend all those things to himself and suddenly felt the weakness of what he was defending. There was nothing to defend." In the end, Ilyich, a defeated man, cries out, "What if my whole life has been wrong?"

If you do not want to end up like Ivan Ilyich, looking back on a life that never came close to your expectations, then you need to ask yourself, Are you ready to be courageous enough not just to recognize life's challenges, but to embrace them and rise above them?

As I have learned, and as I hope you will learn, the very things that afflict us—from divorce to professional defeat, from illness to the loss of a loved one—are actually the very things that can call forth our greatest drive and passion. Through the process of facing our problems and then trying to deal with them, we ultimately make ourselves better human beings.

This is not a two-bit motivational speech. This is a vital, invaluable piece of truth. As Dr. M. Scott Peck writes in his powerful book, *The Road Less Traveled,* "It is in this whole process of meeting and solving problems that life has its meaning. Problems are the cutting edge that distinguishes between success and failure. Problems call forth our courage and our wisdom; indeed, they create our courage and our wisdom."

Granted, I wasn't thinking too much about courage and wisdom when I found myself in that hospital bed. But I'll never forget the first moment when I realized I did not have to be so afraid of the struggle that life was bringing me. It happened when my fiancée, Dallas, came to see me in the hospital. Initially, when she had gotten the phone call that I had been in an accident, she said to her parents, "Oh, he'll be fine, he'll be fine." She thought I was invincible. On an earlier trip between Utah and California, my car had hit a patch of black ice and slid out of control, off the road, flipping onto its side and continuing to slide for another hundred feet. Then it flipped back to its proper position, and I realized I had been untouched. Dallas thought I was invincible—as did I, for that matter. We used to laugh about my earlier childhood brushes with disasters in which I had emerged unharmed. At the age of twelve, for instance, I had tried to parachute from the roof of our two-story home by grasping the four corners of a bed sheet and jumping. About the time I passed the balcony, I realized I was not slowing down. Still, I ended up with just a wounded ego.

So it was no wonder that Dallas said, "Art will be okay." Just the day before, she had been on the phone with me, heard me say "Merry Christmas" and that I could not wait to be with her. The last words she had told me before I had left were, "Be careful, Art. I need you." I promised that everything would be fine.

But then she heard that this time the accident was no laughing matter. My neck had been broken, she was told, and no one was sure what would happen next. Frantic, Dallas caught the first flight to Las Vegas from Utah.

Dallas was my sweetheart, the girl of all my boyhood dreams. For the previous five years, we had laughed together, had fun together, experienced life together, and dreamed together. I had met her when I was just sixteen and she merely fifteen. I had come to Utah with my family for a ski trip, and when we initially got together, we could tell this was going to be more than just another teenage crush. As soon as I got back to California from the ski trip, we inundated each other with phone calls and letters. (I could have used the Internet then!)

In August 1983, when I was twenty-one years old, I asked her to marry me. She said yes, and we began making plans for a wedding. To be together meant everything to us. It seemed at times as though every dollar we made was being spent to fulfill that end. We were either talking long distance on the phone, sending cards and letters (we could have used e-mail back then), or spending our money to make trips back and forth to Utah and California. When we were together, we felt happiest. Our hearts were light and our spirits soared. Every moment together was a new thrill in discovery and understanding. It seemed that the more we were together, the more we wanted to stay that way forever. She made me feel important, like a king. She told me that to love me was the greatest joy of her life.

And now she found herself being guided toward the intensive care wing of Las Vegas Valley Medical Hospital and into my room. She saw my body, covered in a tangle of tubes and hoses, scrapes and blood. She looked at the huge metal tongs attached to the sides of my head with the thirty pounds of weight hung from a traction bar.

My eyes had been only half-open, making the world I looked out on undulate like an underwater movie. When my door had silently opened, I heard the spill in from the busy nurses' station down the hall, I didn't even try to see who was there. I assumed it was another hospital staffer.

And then the face of Dallas moved into focus out of the blur. A knot in my stomach moved up to my throat and stuck; then the knot seemed to come rolling out of my eyes in hot tears. "Hello, sweetheart," were the only words I could muster before more tears began to cloud my vision.

But after standing there for a moment, she took my hand in hers. "Oh, Art, my love," she said.

Here she was, this beautiful young woman, just nineteen years old, arriving to see her fiancé, and I looked so pathetic. How, I wondered, would she ever be able to love me now? How could she even look at me? How could I bring light and joy back into her life and take her away from this awful sight and smell of pain? I felt as if I was disappearing behind a veil of tears. I felt unable to do anything except grieve for all that I thought was lost.

But as she stared at me, it was as if a soft light filled the room. The glow was so gentle, so tender, so full of grace—and so comforting. "Art, we will get through this," Dallas said.

I don't even think she knew just how propehetic her words would be. But today, Dallas and I really do thank God that life has been hard—because we know it's in times of loneliness, discouragement, frustration, and rejection that we begin to learn. When we learn, we grow. And when we grow, the greatest of all miracles happens: We begin to change.

THREE

✺

Do You Find Yourself Asking Why?

Anytime painful events come into our lives, one of the first questions we ask is, "Why?"

Why did this happen to me? Why now? Why, God, why?

We ask "why" about so many things that happen to us, big and small. Why do bad things happen to good people? Why do innocent children suffer? Why can't I ever seem to get ahead? Why don't I get paid what I am worth? Why doesn't anyone like me? Why doesn't my spouse love me? Why am I bored? Why does everything I eat turn to fat?

Believe me, I had my share of "why" questions. I turned my eyes upward again and again, and in my heart I asked why I, an ordinary human, should be bearing such an extraordinary burden of pain and grief. Why I was the one picked to deal with such a tortuous twist of fate? It all seemed so unjust. I had reached a point where I had to get answers to some questions that were inside me. Shutting myself into the world of my heart and mind, I wondered, "Why? Why? Why?"

In a very real sense, my days at Las Vegas Valley Medical were a living hell. When I was wheeled through those swinging emergency room doors, I was greeted by a staff of nurses who were confused and inexperienced when it came to someone suffering from such extensive injuries.

After ten days in Las Vegas, four of which were spent in intensive care, I was taken by ambulance to a local airport. Gingerly, my stretcher was loaded into a small single-engine plane. The plane taxied down the runway and took off, and the pilot banked the plane gently to the right to give me my last look at Las Vegas. I was then flown west toward new horizons, to the Santa Clara Valley Medical Center in San Jose, California, which specialized in spinal cord injuries.

Valley Medical was a county-run facility. It wasn't the nicest place, and it wouldn't win any awards for the way it smelled. The floors were yellowed linoleum leading to walls painted a cheerless green. My whole room hummed as a new group of doctors, nurses, and attendants busily made their way in and out of the room. As doctors came to my bed, they would look here, poke there, ask me if I could feel this or that, and then hurry out again. I soon learned that the constant flow of activity in the new hospital was the norm, day and night. At least every two hours around the clock for the next four months, somebody would wake me to take my blood pressure, temperature, and vital signs. If sleep and good rest were what I needed, I had come to the wrong place.

My new doctor came in and introduced himself as Dr. Kelly. He had a strong Irish accent and was difficult to understand. I could tell he was a leader among the other doctors, and his presence commanded respect. He was a man well acquainted with the pain and suffering of others. He had assisted thousands of unfortunate people dealing with spinal cord injuries.

He had many notable qualities as a doctor, but I soon learned that tact and sensitivity were not among them. To put it mildly, his bedside manner was awful. Within the first couple of days of my stay at Valley Medical Hospital, Dr. Kelly called a special family conference. He outlined some of the new policies at the hospital and related how he saw the future for all of us. He also announced his personal plan of action for me. For one thing, he said, visiting hours would be strictly limited and adhered to, regardless of any special needs.

Second, he stated abruptly, it was to be understood that I would never walk again. Period. I would be required to have constant help for the rest of my life, and I would always be in a wheelchair. So let's not waste time, said Dr. Kelly, by talking about me walking. There would be no such discussion.

I understood his honesty. Yet nothing he did left much feeling for hope, or even the slightest sense of goodwill. It wasn't that I expected him to say, "You will walk." But it was hard to forgive his insensitivity to our feelings, and the lack of attention he paid to the questions of those close to me who wanted to help and needed to understand.

Finally, Dr. Kelly said, I would begin therapy as soon as I could get up from my bed, which would require him to install a halo brace on me within the next couple of days.

This wasn't the kind of halo that encircles the heads of saints and angels. I am speaking of a halo brace used in hospitals—and there is absolutely nothing angelic about it.

At first, I objected to the idea of a halo brace. I saw little need to wear one of those hideous things. However, he insisted it was in my best interests for me to do what he said. I was told that with the halo brace I'd be able to get up into a wheelchair and begin rehabilitation immediately. I still hesitated. Unless you've seen a halo brace, you may have a hard time understanding why I would be so reluctant.

The halo brace starts with a large breastplate made of plastic and lined with sheepskin to keep the plastic from irritating the skin. Steel bars are attached to the chest plate and extend up and over the shoulders and then down the back. From the bars over the shoulders, another steel bar goes up along each side of the head. This bar is connected to the infamous halo. The halo is a flat metal bar about one inch wide that completely encircles the head from the front to the back. If you've got that pictured, then imagine four three-inch bolts, pointed sharply at the end, screwed into the patient's head, two in the front and two in the back, to hold the halo in place. Gruesome, isn't it?

In fact, even today I get chills and feel weak when I see one. The halo brace is almost medieval in appearance, frightening to look at. It made me seem as if I was in a cage.

You bet I hesitated having it put on. And in retrospect, if I could make the decision again, taking into account the excruciating pain, discomfort, and inability to rest and the awful look of the whole thing, I would definitely have made sure it was not put on me. Although the brace is essential in some cases, it turned out that it would not have been a necessity for me after all.

Still, the doctor's assistant came into my room, carrying the halo. Silently, I wondered if I would have the strength it would take to endure the installation process. I knew those three-inch bolts would have to be manually screwed into my skull through my forehead and just behind my ears. What I didn't know was that it would be done with no anesthesia.

The doctor did inject medication—some kind of painkiller, he called it—in each of the four areas the bolts were to enter, but whatever it was supposed to do, it didn't. As he and his assistants strapped the breastplate into place and adjusted the hardware, one of the bolts scraped across an area of the forehead where it was to be inserted. The pain cut through me like a lumber saw! I told Dr. Kelly that I thought that area was supposed to be numb from the "painkiller," but it wasn't. He continued adjusting the breastplate and hardware. I told him again, this time with panic in my voice. "Please!" I begged him, "wait until the anesthesia has taken effect!" Ignoring my pleas, he had somebody hold my arms down, and he picked up the instrument to be used for screwing in the bolts. He commented coldly, "It's supposed to hurt. It'll go away." And then he began the arduously slow process of inserting them into my skull.

Never have I felt anything so painful in all my life. I cannot conceive of anything more excruciating. I felt as though an explosion was going off inside my body. I wanted to die. I wanted life to stop right then. Surely, I thought, I could not suffer this intensely and survive. Tears were forced from the corners of my eyes. My face became contorted and wracked in pain. I felt as if the horror would never end.

"Go ahead, scream if you want to," Dr. Kelly said as he continued. I would have, but I couldn't. I opened my mouth and nothing would come out. My vision began to go black. I knew my body was beginning to go into shock. The doctors backed away from me to observe what they had done. I heard Dr. Kelly say casually, "He's in some pain. I think we need to give him something for it."

Some pain? My world was spinning and I lost all recognition of what was going on around me. Everything went dark.

Again, I wondered, "Why me?" Why this extra suffering? Was this some way God decided to punish me? Was this to purge me of my pride and arrogance? To make me a better, more sensitive person? Was there some lesson here to help me cure my faults?

Perhaps you haven't been through something as physically extreme as I have, but that doesn't mean you aren't plagued by the "why" question. It's probably why you have bought this book: you're asking why something has happened to you. It could be the loss of a loved one or the loss of a job, the betrayal by a spouse or by a friend, the disappointment of a child gone astray or a business venture gone bust. Your "why" question is no different than mine. Why, you have asked, did this have to happen? Why did you have to go through an experience that left you so devastated?

I could spend the rest of the book trying to grapple with the question of why we experience misfortune—a question that is of especially intense interest to me because of my devout belief in God. But I will tell you now, if you are looking for a satisfying answer about why we suffer, you have come to the wrong place. If you are looking for a reason why God doesn't step in and prevent more suffering, I do not completely know. I do believe that God does not cause our misfortunes. Some misfortunes are just a matter of bad luck, others are caused by bad people, some are caused by our own destructive actions, and some are the consequences of living in a world with natural laws. The fact is that there are going to be times when we all suffer and we do not understand why.

Which leads me to a very important step I believe you must take to begin your journey back from whatever it is that has afflicted you: Don't ask why.

That's it—simple and potent. It sounds strange, I know, but asking "why" ultimately gets you nowhere because ultimately you're never going to understand why you suffer. And think about this: If you did find the long-sought-after answer, would it solve your problem? Of course not. You can't control the "why" to your suffering. All you can control is what the suffering does to you and what sort of person you become because of it. Will you become depressed, bitter, and angry? Or will you use the pain to become better, stronger, fuller?

The question about your own trials and tribulations, then, should not focus on why they have happened. The question should be where your trials and tribulations can take you. The question for you should be what kind of meaning those trials and tribulations can give your life.

Now let me be very honest. No matter what I say, I know you're going to ask the "why" question, just as I asked it after my accident. It's a given. And I'm certainly not faulting you for asking the question. But at some point, if you want to move forward, you have to stop asking why. You've got to come to some place in your own mind where you stop obsessing about why something happened to you.

Perhaps this will help you stop asking the "why" question. Instead of asking why people have to suffer, try to imagine a world in which there is no suffering whatsoever. People don't get sick, people don't feel pain, and people don't die. There is no old age, no hard times, no trials of our faith, no misunderstandings, no errors, no mistakes.

Is that the perfect world? No, it sounds like a kind of plastic hell.

Oscar Wilde once wrote, "When the gods want to punish us they answer our prayers." Consider the things people normally pray for, and see if a culmination of all those desires granted by God upon the human race as a whole would not lead to misery itself. If there were no misery, could there be true joy? If there were no pain, could there be real gratitude or comfort? If there were no death, would we ever really savor life? If there were no struggle, would we ever grow? If we did not grow, would we ever reach our highest potential?

We can only experience love and joy to the extent that we have experienced pain and tragedy. Pain not only can enrich us, it can teach us. If you were to put your hand into a fire, what would you do? Pull it out, I hope. The cause of the pain is immediately understood and the message is very clear: "Stop doing what you are doing!" Sometimes, however, the source of the pain you and I experience in our personal lives—in our relationships, in our dealings with financial security, and in our emotions—is not so evident. Failing to understand, we often continue to do the same things over and over again. And we wonder why the pain never goes away.

What would happen if you left your hand in the fire for three days? The answer is obvious: You'd lose your hand. I don't mean to be morbid, but there is a significant point to be made here. When your hand is gone, will it hurt anymore? No. The wrist may be uncomfortable, but when the hand is gone, it will no longer hurt. The point is this: If we ignore pain long enough, it will eventually go away. But by the time it does, we may have caused lasting and permanent damage, and a new pain will enter our lives, which is often worse than the first.

Not long after my accident, for instance, I laid a steaming hot plate of food on my lap. I noticed nothing for a minute or two, then I started smelling something burning. I looked at my food. It hadn't been overcooked. I looked around the room. I couldn't see anything on fire. Then I looked down again and discovered the source of the odor. The hot plate was burning my skin. I was smelling my own burning flesh.

I received serious burns on both my thighs. The wounds were ugly, but I had no sensation of pain—one of the dubious benefits of being paralyzed. And pain is important. It acts as a warning. It tells us that we are damaging ourselves in some way. What if we could cut our finger on a knife with no discomfort? Without the sensation of pain, I had done serious damage to my body. If I had enjoyed even the slightest suggestion of discomfort, I could have avoided costly medical bills and weeks of inconvenience and concern.

Pain also can redirect us. Because I am an avid animal lover with a particular fondness for dogs, I once decided to buy two rottweilers. One weighed 100 pounds and the other 120 pounds, and they loved to show their affection. But they did three things over a short period of time that motivated me to take dramatic measures in their lives. First, I came home one day to discover that my living room couch was in the family room. When your dogs move major pieces of furniture, that's a problem. Second, I took both of my dogs for a walk one day. Before starting out, I tied both of their leashes to my wheelchair. Then they saw a cat. Suddenly, I was Ben-Hur, racing wildly down the sidewalk in my chariot! Needless to say, I didn't do that again. Third, although my rottweilers may not have been very bright, they were extremely intelligent (there is definitely a difference). They figured out that I was in a wheelchair. So anytime I got angry at them, they would run for the nearest curb, jump on it, and smile! That really ticked me off.

To control the dogs better, I invested in a couple of shock collars. The purpose of shock collars, frankly, is to inflict pain (even if the pain only turns out to be a slight irritation.) And let me tell you, there is an appropriate time to zap a rottweiler through the shock collar. For instance, when my larger dog, who I am convinced had a personality disorder, decided that small children are hairless cats—he liked chasing them—the time definitely had come to shock him.

Why inflict pain through the shock collars? A practical reason was that I wanted my dogs to associate the pain with their behavior and not with me. If I was forced to discipline my dogs personally, I would either yell at them, swat them, or chase after them. They would do one of several things—run from me, cower, or bite me—none of which was acceptable. By using the shock collars as a form of discipline, my dogs associated the pain or discomfort with their behavior and not with me. They assumed some big dog in the sky was doing it to them. What's more, if the dogs associated the pain with their behavior and not with me, then they were much more obedient even when I was away.

But the biggest reason was that the pain got my dogs to change their behavior. Lest you think that I am cruel for using shock collars, let me ask you a question. When our children exhibit behaviors that are inappropriate, dangerous, or just rude, isn't it often necessary in order to correct them to introduce some form of discomfort, even pain, into their lives? The pain can be provided in a variety of ways. We scold them—which is, of course, a form of emotional pain. Or we spank them—physical pain. Or we send them to their rooms or take away with their privileges—I guess we'd call that freedom pain. Would you agree that if some form of discomfort is not applied, children frequently do not learn?

This is an important point to understand. I don't believe we are put through hard times in order to learn a lesson that we couldn't learn some other way. But if we never get off the "why" question, if we never get unstuck from the idea that life is unfair to us, then we will never have a healthy response to living. We'll remain very frustrated, anxious, angry, and irritable. We'll buy into all the reactions that take away our inner peace and eat away at us.

In essence, we become what I call I "why-ners." Our constant barrage of why's sounds a lot like whining to me. If you are a "why-ner," you're not looking for solutions. You are not interested in answers. You only want sympathy. But if you stop "why-ning," you can develop a belief system that says there are unfair things that happen in life that are an integral part of existence, and that when they happen you'll deal with them the best you can. Only then are you in the position to start making changes in your life.

FOUR

Rather Than Looking for Someone to Blame,
Look for Something to Change ...
About Yourself

After the halo brace was put on me at the Santa Clara Valley Medical Center in San Jose, California, I was able to begin my rehabilitation program, although the size and weight of the brace made exercise difficult and cumbersome. Sleeping at night was strained at best. I felt as if I was sleeping on pencils. Headaches became a daily event. My head felt like a bruised melon in a closed vise.

Three times each day my tong sites had to be sterilized in order to avoid infection where the bolts entered my head. It was never a comfortable procedure, and usually I just gritted my teeth and endured. Many of the nurses and attendants were sensitive to my discomfort and did everything they could to make the experience less painful for me. These were special people who, even though they lived among pain every day, had managed to stay sensitive to their patients and had learned to persistently exercise compassion.

There was one male nurse who was different from the rest. His eyes were dark and deep-set. He always reeked of cigarette smoke, and sometimes of alcohol. He was generally an unclean person with language to match. His life seemed entirely void of anything called compassion.

In fact, he seemed to enjoy seeing others in pain. For some sadistic reason, he would think it was funny if I jerked back in pain when he hit a sensitive spot or if he scrubbed too hard. As the weeks went on, his care of my wounds became rougher and rougher. Finally, one day, when I felt I had taken as much as I could, I asked him to let someone else clean my tong sites. He refused, calling me names that were both cruel and inappropriate. When I told him I would not allow him to scrub me again without me talking to my doctor, he laughed, held my weak arms to the bed, and scrubbed mercilessly.

It is still hard for me to imagine that kind of cruelty. I find it difficult to believe that it could ever have happened. I laid awake at night, furious at what this man was doing to me. I found myself blaming him for so much of my pain. How was I to resolve these feelings of hurt and anger? How was I going to forgive such things?

In the end, there was only one thing I had to do—and it is what you have to do, too, in your own journey. I had to stop blaming other people or other things for what was happening to me.

I'm not saying people should not be held accountable for their hurtful behavior. But the only thing blaming does is to keep the focus off you. It means you aren't dealing with your problems.

The practice of blaming has become commonplace in our

modern world, even though it eventually stunts our emotional growth. I call this epidemic "the Apple Syndrome." To understand the Apple Syndrome, you have to go back thousands of years with me to a beautiful garden in a place called Eden. Adam and Eve had been strictly forbidden to partake of the fruit of the tree of knowledge of good and evil. But they did eat the apple, and the consequences were not far behind. The Lord went to Adam and in essence asked, "Why, Adam? Why did you eat of the fruit of the tree?" And what did Adam say? "That woman!" (I'm taking a little poetic license here.) "That woman caused me to eat it." The Lord turned to Eve and asked, "Eve, why did you eat of the fruit of the tree?" Eve's response? "The serpent beguiled me!"

By believing that they could always "blame" their behavior on someone else, Adam and Eve made a serious mistake. They forfeited the chance for a much more fulfilling life. Similarly, when we fall victim to the Apple Syndrome by attempting to shift responsibility for our lives to outside circumstances, we deny ourselves opportunities to learn and to grow. When we point fingers of blame, what we are saying is that we have little or no control over our destiny. Instead of focusing on ourselves, we focus on others, stating, "When they change, I'll change." We say other things like, "If only she would be more supportive," or "I'll never get ahead as long as he's around," or "If they just hadn't kept pushing me." Each of these statements puts us into a mental condition of surrendering to circumstance and resigning ourselves to fate.

I do not mean to imply that outside circumstances or other people do not play a role in our lives. Certainly, many factors influence the conditions we experience. But if we focus our attention solely upon those factors, we feed a spirit of fear and uncertainty regarding our future.

———

When it comes to blame, a lot of people have asked me about my feelings toward John, the driver. I am asked often how I was able to get over my anger toward him. People tell me that he was, after all, the one who was technically at fault. How can I not blame him? The fact was that physically, John was not badly hurt. He received only minor cuts, abrasions, and a puncture wound in his bicep. "Doesn't that bother you?" some people have even asked. "Doesn't it seem unfair that he sustained less injuries than you did?"

That is an awkward question, because John never did anything to me. What happened was an accident—not an act of negligence or disregard or insensitivity. Just an accident. As many friends heard of my accident and rushed to my side, all too often John's pain went unnoticed. But John did not spend his time feeling sorry for himself, or running off to hide. Day and night he stayed by my bedside. I'll never forget those first days, John always standing there in the doorway in his bloodstained white pants, his head drooping, his face empty. He helped me, he read to me, he tried to bring me comfort. I knew he would have traded places with me in an instant.

A few months after the accident, I was allowed to travel with Dallas to the wedding of Dallas's brother, Scott. Scott and I had become good friends over the years, and it was a special time for all of us. John was also there. John and Scott were new friends, and he desired to share in this special event.

The ceremony was beautiful and touching. Dallas and I looked across at each other with tear-filled eyes as the ceremony began. We were both reminded of our own interrupted marriage plans: a long and flowing white dress still hung, unused and covered with plastic, in Dallas's closet back home. This day, I thought for a moment, should be my wedding day. Dallas and I should be the ones kneeling at that altar. Only now I couldn't even kneel.

I am not sure if John saw our eyes and interpreted the hurt and emotional pain of the moment, or whether he had just been touched by the whole experience himself, but silently, he began to cry. Tears streamed down his face for the rest of the ceremony. When it was over, he excused himself.

We finally found him in another room of the church. There, in the quiet confines of that sacred edifice, he was weeping uncontrollably. His whole body jerked as he gasped for air, and then he cried some more. I have never seen anyone break down with such intensity and pain. He seemed completely overwhelmed. We tried to help restore him, to assure and comfort him, but he was inconsolable. His heart was breaking—a heart he thought had been healed months ago. As many times as I told him that the accident was not his fault, that he in no way intended to harm me and therefore is not to be blamed or held responsible, the terror of what happened continued to haunt him. In so many ways, the "tragedy" that the accident created in my life was no more distressing and painful than the nightmare that John still lives with today.

I know that no one would have blamed me if I had blamed John for my condition. No one would even have blamed me if I had blamed God. No one would have blamed me if I had blamed life in general. No one would have said to me, "Hey, you know what, Art? Other people have had it worse." Let's be honest: I had it pretty bad. But what I realized was that no matter how much I found fault with another, and regardless how much time I spent blaming that person for my problems, it was not going to change me.

Let me share with you a parable I wrote about the baggage of hurt, bitterness, and anger that we carry through much of our lives.

A man walked along a dusty highway. In a short while he came upon a small community. He was hot, tired, and thirsty, and he began to search for a resting place.

In his search, he found a group of people who were unwilling to help him. They were intolerant and selfish. Rather than tend to his needs, they sent him on his way, unsatisfied. The man stood at the far edge of town. Looking back, he gently picked up a rough stone from the highway, placed it in his bag, and said to himself, "I'll remember this."

As he traveled farther, he came upon a gathering of people beside the highway. They all wore the finest clothing and jewelry that one could possibly desire. The man had traveled long without companionship and was hungry for human conversation. He would rest here a while, acquaint himself with these good people, and then be on his way again.

As he approached, someone from the group caught a glimpse of him and began to laugh and point. The others looked, and they too laughed at the man whose clothes were torn, dirty, and old. The man hung his head and traveled on. A short distance later, he reached down and picked up another stone, this one larger than the first, and placed it in his bag, saying, "I'll remember this."

Finally, unable to go any farther without rest, he sat beneath the shade of a big tree and slept. Upon awakening, he found that someone had stolen all his possessions except the bag with the stones. Quickly, he found another large stone and placed it in his bag and moved on, repeating, "I'll remember this." These stones became the only thing that this man carried. Each day, he took his stones from the bag to count and clean. Each day, as he suffered more cruelties, he gathered more stones to add to his growing collection.

At last, one day, he found he could go no farther. His bag was full and heavy and difficult to carry. Yet even then, his stones had become too important for him to leave. They had become the center of his life. He cared for these stones, talked of them in his conversations with others, and used them to justify his own acts of misbehavior. What would he do without them?

So he continued to carry them. His back became bent with the weight as he strained through life collecting these stones. His eyes became cynical, and his body showed signs of early aging. But he could not give up his stones. Finally, in frustration, he died.

How different would this man's life have been without those stones? How much easier would his way have been, and how much lighter his load to bear?

When a crisis comes in our life, we all have this choice to carry stones. To hate and to blame would be so easy. But in the end, those who collect stones as a reminder of past wrongdoings find themselves carrying far greater weights than the very people who have done them wrong. When it came to the male nurse, I realized that the weight of my adversities was already heavy enough. I could not consider the thought of adding more by carrying the burden of his unkindness or injustice as well. I desired to leave his stone along the highway where I had found it. This is no different than you carrying the stone of blame toward your boss, for example. You blame him for what has happened to you. Instead of plotting how you can sharpen your own management skills, you paralyze yourself by coming up with reasons why your boss is at fault.

I know that breaking the cycle of blame is not easy—to the contrary. When I lay in that hospital bed, I knew for the first time in my life—intellectually and emotionally—that I had a right to be angry. I was wearing my seat belt. We drove the speed limit on long, deserted desert roads. I was a God-fearing, Christian man who was true to his covenants. And here I was cheated. It was hard not to keep looking for someone to blame. I found it necessary to continually persist, to continue expressing and developing my desire to be free from hate and anger.

Do you know what ultimately would have resulted if I had kept the blame game going? Do you know what would have resulted from me blaming someone who has burdens of his own? (And as I hope you know, even the diabolical male nurse has his own burdens.) In the end, no one would have wanted to be around me. At first they would have felt an obligation to be at my side and console me. But they wouldn't have wanted to spend much time around me if I angrily complained nonstop about how I was being mistreated. They would, however, be more willing to help a person who was first trying to help himself.

Try this exercise: Make a list of whatever is going wrong in your life, from the biggest events to the most trivial items, and then beside that list write down everything and everyone you want to blame for that particular problem. For instance, let's say you think you're too fat. If you want to blame it on McDonald's cheeseburgers, then write that down. Perhaps you just don't normally feel well. If you want to blame that feeling on a bad doctor or on the pollen in the air, then write that down. Maybe you can't find a suitable partner. If you want to blame that on the argument that "men are creeps," then write that down.

Now look at your list. Ask yourself if you are any different now that you know exactly what or who to blame, and then ask yourself if that has helped you come up with a more constructive program to solve your problems.

Not a very positive picture, is it? Wouldn't it be better simply to decide to eliminate all blame from your life and focus instead on what you can do to rid yourself of the unhappiness that afflicts you? Wouldn't it be better to evaluate all the stones that you are carrying in your own bag of life—your stones of resentment, anger, and spite?

Blaming will not change you. It only gives you some shallow justification for continuing to look outside yourself, rather than turning inward and rebuilding your life. When I started throwing my stones away, I began to feel a greater sense of peace. Most importantly, I began to get to a point where instead of looking for someone to blame, I began looking for something to change. I began asking, "What can I change in myself? What can I do differently?"

FIVE

✳

Do You Live in the Past and/or in the Future?

This is another of those thorny questions that you must ask yourself before you begin your journey: Are you living in the present?

It's a simplistic question, I know, but a vital one. One of the distinguishing characteristics of people who remain miserable is that they do a lot of what I call "time traveling." They either spend much of their time thinking about or brooding over what has happened to them in the past, or they are consumed with whatever it is that may happen tomorrow.

It is easy in this culture to deemphasize the now and travel either backward or forward in time. We live in a world that, on one hand, constantly asks us to reanalyze why we didn't pursue certain options in our past or to study what might have happened to us a long time ago that kept us from being our best. On the other hand, we're also constantly being reminded to think about tomorrow. We're asked to picture what our lives might be like in the future.

Do you know people who keep traveling through their pasts? They talk about how they are a product of a "dysfunctional family" or how they've never been the same since someone did something bad to them. Do you, likewise, know people who can't get their minds off the future, no matter what they achieve, how much money they earn, or how many blessings come their way? They incessantly believe that they still have more to do before they can call themselves happy. These are the people who, during the midst of a wonderful vacation, will spend much of their time thinking about all the things they should be doing back home. Or they worry about bills that are soon to come due, or relationships that might explode.

It seems so impossible to believe that your best time in life exists at no other time and in no other place than the present. But this is another vital part of your strategy that you must have in order to rebuild a better life: You must let go of what's happened, forget about what could happen, and take charge of your present. There is only one moment in which you can experience anything, and that moment is "now," so don't throw away your time by dwelling on past or future experiences, by living in moments other than the current ones. Henry David Thoreau's oft-quoted comment, "I went to the woods because I wished to live deliberately, to front only the essential facts of life, and see if I could not learn what it had to teach, and not, when I come to die, discover that I had not lived," originated from his awareness that his preoccupation with the yesterdays and tomorrows of his life was not real living at all. He realized that with his mind on past events or on unknown tomorrows, the glory and beauty of what was happening right before him was muted. He realized that only through immersion in the present was life encountered and lived. For Thoreau, real living was the experience of what was immediately before him.

An attitude that avoids enjoyment today only means an evasion of happiness forever. Happiness becomes something for tomorrow and therefore ever elusive.

Does this seem like an impossible task: to exist emotionally, intellectually, and spiritually in the present? To stop wondering what life would be like in a different circumstance and be completely attentive to the moment you're in now?

Let me put it another way. Do you realize how much you are punishing yourself when you remain a prisoner of your past or your future? Do you understand that when you spend too much time in the past or future, you're only making yourself feel overwhelmed, discouraged, frustrated, and unhappy?

The famous short story "The Eighty-Yard Run," by Irwin Shaw, is about a college freshman who, at his first football practice, breaks loose for an eighty-yard touchdown run. His teammates look at him with awe. His coach predicts great things for him. His girlfriend picks him up after practice and kisses him. He has a feeling right then that life is completely satisfying. But nothing in his life ever lives up to that day. He is not that great a football player. After college, he is not that great a businessman. His marriage sours and he cannot stop thinking about that day years ago. He cannot get out of the past enough to start a better present.

On the other hand, in one of the classic works of world literature, the dramatic poem *Faust,* the hero of the poem is so worried that he is not experiencing enough joy and success and respect that he makes a bargain with the devil just to get a guarantee of a better future. Too late, he discovers that what really matters is what is happening to him in the present. "Let this moment linger, it is so good," the tragic Dr. Faust laments.

Well, you're wondering, should you forget about the past and future altogether? Of course not. If you don't know certain things about your past, you're destined to repeat them. And there is nothing more motivating than the hope for a better future. But let this be a warning: Too much thinking about the past or present can be harmful to your health.

I spend very little time thinking about my past. It isn't because it isn't valuable to me. To the contrary, there are experiences I will never forget. However, as good or as bad as yesterday may have been, it is unchangeable. There is nothing I can do to bring it back. It is impossible to relive it, other than in my mind. So even though the old slogan "Hindsight is 20-20" is valuable, it has its limits. There is no way any of us can spend time thinking about or discussing the mistakes we made when we were teenagers, the opportunities we failed to grasp two weeks ago, or the pain we experienced yesterday without sinking into a feeling of depression. Think about some unhappy people you know. What do they talk about? What stories do they tell over and over again? It's always about who offended them in the past or unfair events that once happened to them.

I've often wondered why people hold onto so much pain for so long. They either hold onto mistakes that they have made or will recount endlessly how they've been hurt—a pattern of thinking that can go on for years despite the obvious pain it continues to evoke. The only conclusion I have reached is that some people become so comfortable with the mistakes, abuses, and pain of the past that they don't know how to live without it. It has actually become familiar to them. It gives them something to dwell on. And more than anything, it gives them a reason.

A reason for what? A reason for everything. They can explain everything that's happened to them by pointing to the past. It's because of the past that they are not happy. It is because of the past that they don't have a better job. It is because of the past that they have few friends. It is because of the past that they are financially in trouble or mentally discouraged. Do you get the idea? If those very people decided to disconnect from the past—to actually rid themselves of the anger, abuse, and pain of what's happened before—then what excuse would they have for failing to be happy today? Holding onto the past only prevents them from enjoying today.

I spend very little time reflecting on my future, either. I know there is nothing I can do about tomorrow, other than what I am willing to do today.

This is a critical point to understand. It can give you a whole new way of dealing with disasters or setbacks in your life as well as how you approach your problems. It can also give you an entirely different way to see what happiness really means. You don't have to be told how much time you spend in your pursuit of happiness. If you're like everyone else, you're probably leapfrogging from one activity, relationship, purchase, or job to the next, hoping to find a glimmer of happiness. Or you are marching from one conquest to another, figuring that might give you some enduring contentment. Some of you explore a variety of religions. Others put your hearts and minds into work. Others try vices, from alcohol to promiscuity. You buy any number of toys, from exotic vacation homes to the best clothes.

Be honest: happiness is the great elusive quality in your life, isn't it? That's why you pursue it so diligently. That's why, perhaps, you have bought this book. Happiness is our holy grail. In a poll taken in Asian countries, parents were asked what they wanted most for their children. Overwhelmingly, the response was that they wanted their children to be successful. In America, parents were asked a similar question. Universally, American parents expressed a desire for their children to be . . . happy.

So why, if it's that important, do we keep hitting one dead end after another? I have heard so many people say that, "I'll be happy when I get my new promotion." Or, "I'll be happy when I lose that extra twenty pounds." Or, "I'll be happy when the kids go back to school." The list goes on and on.

This thinking is dangerous because it presupposes that happiness is a "response" to having or doing something that you don't yet have or do. Much of life is driven on the stimulus–response relationship. Here's an example. "Stimulus" is when a dog barks at you and bares his teeth. "Response" is when your heart beats faster, your palms get sweaty, and you prepare to run. In the same way, most people believe our happiness can only be the response to a certain stimulus. People think that an expensive car—a stimulus—will lead to a response of happiness. If they have a great-paying job—the proper stimulus, they believe—then their response will be happiness.

But what if the opposite is true? What if happiness is the stimulus and the response is whatever life brings from that happiness?

Think about it. When we are happy, we have closer friends and more loving relationships, simply because people want to be around us. When we are happy, we naturally take better care of our bodies instead of abusing them. When we are happy, we tend to have more success in our work. People who behave in successful ways are people who already feel good about themselves.

I want you to try a test that I once gave myself. Finish the question, "I'll be happy when . . ." And don't just limit yourself to one answer. Go through everything you think will make you happy—from money to health to family to career.

When I did the test, I wrote down nearly 100 things. I decided

I would be happy when I was out of debt, when I had written a book, when I had spoken to an audience of 10,000 people, and on and on. It was basically a dream list. I included some very personal things that were related to my accident. I figured I'd be happy if I could put on my pants by myself, if I could hold a fork, if I could learn to drive again.

Then, over the next few weeks, I went back to the list and asked myself, "Do I really need to do this one thing to be genuinely happy?" The answer, of course, was always no, and I'd eliminate that particular item from the list. Needless to say, by the time I was done, I had eliminated everything.

I thought for a while about what I had learned from that exercise, and clearly, one thing emerged. The fewer the "I'll-be-happy-when" items on my list meant the easier it would be to be happier. In the end, I whittled my list down to one item: every day that I'm above this ground is a good day. For me, every day I was above ground (i.e., not dead) meant that I was happy. As a result, I began having a lot of good days in a row. My happiness wasn't dependent on my having something or having achieved something. My happiness was based on the fact that I was alive, and it didn't matter what the circumstances were. And it was because I chose happiness that other good fortune began coming to me. I didn't let anxiety, disappointment, and frustration get in the way of my life. Hey, I was able to put on my pants eventually.

Truly happy people spend most of their time on today. Why? Because today is all we have. Yesterday is gone and tomorrow never comes. Yes, there are lessons to be learned from the past. Yes, tomorrow gives us hope to endure. But happiness can be found only when we focus on today. Otherwise, when the future does arrive, it becomes our new present, which means we, once again, start obsessing about a new future. It's a vicious circle.

So ask yourself, "What am I holding onto? What pain from the past do I use as an excuse for unhappiness today?" Then ask yourself what fears of the future you hold onto as well.

As I travel the world speaking with young and old alike, I've noticed the diminishing self-confidence so many of you are experiencing. Your lack of self-confidence translates itself into your occupations, personal relationships, and spiritual growth. You often feel an overwhelming sense of hopelessness and uncertainty about who you are. This is the reason I see more and more of you time-travel, or turn to the Apple Syndrome and blame others, or wallow in self-pity by asking nothing but "why" questions.

Psychologists have taught us that self-confidence stems from perceived control. When we perceive that we control our destiny, happiness, and spiritual future, we tend to have greater confidence in ourselves and in our world. The greatest damage of time traveling is that you are not giving yourself the chance to get back into the driver's seat, to take 100 percent responsibility for your own life. If you do not realize that everything is up to you—everything!—then you are going to fail. It is only when you are ready and willing to take responsibility that it will be possible to make significant, lasting change. The only thing you do by looking outside yourself for answers or for excuses is to surrender your own power.

But when you perceive that you control your destiny, only then will you find the confidence in yourself to change your life. Only then will you be able to strip away all your defenses and fears, raise your standards of personal excellence to what will seem to be wildly unreasonable levels, and learn to stay diligently on course so that you may advance in the direction of your greatest dreams.

You will know what steps to take to move up in your life, what to do when conflict develops, and most important, how to get back on course when you feel yourself slipping. You will find your career advancing to the next level, you will get your most creative juices flowing, you will forever alter the way you raise your children and treat your spouse and give back to your community. And you will do all these things not because you feel you ought to, but because you choose, because you want to, because you're ready to push yourself to the limits of your abilities, to defy the naysayers and ultimately to feel that bone-deep sense of satisfaction that you lived life to its fullest.

If you are looking for something to read that will act like a salve on your emotional wounds, making you feel better right now, then I recommend that you give this book to someone else—because I want to shake you to your very core, to wake you up, to make you stop sleepwalking and start fighting for real change that lasts. This book is a clarion call to action—an unapologetic command that you must take charge of your life today, that you must be William Ernest Henley when he wrote, in the midst of his despair, "I am the master of my fate; I am the captain of my soul."

In fact, your chance to win is right here, right now—not in the past, and not in the future. As one ancient philosopher once put it, "Today is the first day of the rest of your life." Never forget that God has given every single one of us the most astonishing uniqueness. There's no one in the world who can do what you can do, who can think and see the way you do, who can create what you can create. You are a complex mesh of finely woven styles, viewpoints, abilities, tastes, and gifts. If you don't get to live your life, you've lost an incalculable treasure.

If you are still a doubting Thomas, wondering whether you really do have the ability to handle life's biggest problems, I ask you to read on. Let the book unfold. In these last few chapters, you have learned the importance of setting aside your excuses. Now, with each successive chapter, you will be given specific tools to give yourself a winning chance.

Now let's get our lives moving.

PART THREE

Overcoming Your

Paralysis

*Uncommon Strategies for Making
the Impossible Probable*

SIX

✳

Don't Make Your Problems More Than Just That...Problems

STRATEGY: CONTROL YOUR DESTINY BY CONTROLLING
HOW YOU CHOOSE TO RESPOND

When anything takes us out of our normal comfort zones—being fired from our job, becoming the victim of a bad accident, separating from our spouse—our sense of reality can get blown all out of proportion. We experience some kind of mental meltdown. We see whatever challenge faces us as one insurmountable wall. A torrent of negative thoughts starts blowing inside our heads, and we let our minds become ruled by panicky perceptions of what our new reality will be.

After my accident, I had many thoughts that I would be spending the rest of my days in a kind of living hell. I could not imagine my physical paralysis being anything but the deepest burden, not only on me but on anyone who loved me. I felt myself drifting away. I would slip back for a few seconds, only to spiral down again. I pleaded, cried out, wailed in anguish for direction, but I heard nothing, felt nothing. I was so terrified that I couldn't put together a logical thought.

What's more, during my first days in the hospital, there was always someone telling me what I would never do. At one point, I asked the doctors why they were so pessimistic about my future. Their response was, "We just don't want you to get a false sense of hope."

I was silent for a long time. And then something clicked inside me. "No," I said. "All you're doing is giving me a false sense of hopelessness. And that's not the way I'm going to live my life."

It was a breakthrough moment for me. I was not going to let myself be defined by my problems. I was not going to follow the doctors' advice and focus on the enormity of the new life that I had.

"Uh-oh," you're saying, "here it comes. Art's about to do the big speech on the Power of Positive Thinking."

No. As I've already said, I'm not into the standard self-help jargon. I will not try to inspire you simply to think positively and then send you on your way. But here is an undeniable fact: Although we will never be able to keep problems from coming our way, we can choose the way we deal with those problems. We all are going to have bad experiences. What is important is how we interpret those experiences. That's not positive thinking. That's smart thinking.

This idea—the reaction that you can choose the way you respond to whatever has happened to you—is the crux of finding permanent happiness in your life. You probably know the story of Victor Frankl, who after suffering enormous atrocities in Jewish concentration camps under Nazi control in World War II, made this powerful observation: "Everything can be taken away from a man but one thing: the last of all human freedoms—to choose one's attitude in any given set of circumstances, to choose one's own way."

Frankl made that statement in the midst of the worst holocaust in human history. Yet he realized, even then, that there is no such thing as an unfortunate circumstance that could cause one to be unhappy. Happiness and success in life do not depend on circumstances. They depend on what you do with those circumstances. They don't depend on what people tell you your life should be. They depend on what you tell yourself your life should be. That was the key to my being able to build back my life: the recognition that I could choose how to respond to all that had happened to me.

Easier said than done, right? In the midst of tragedy, is it really possible to choose your own reality—to choose happiness? You have grown up in a culture that has taught you that you are not responsible for your feelings and that you certainly cannot control them. You have been taught such phrases as, "I cannot help the way I feel" or "I'm just angry, I can't explain it," or "You're embarrassing me," or "You hurt my feelings." You believe those messages suggest to you that it's always something outside yourself that is causing what you feel. You've grown up believing that anger, fear, and hate—as well as love and joy, for that matter—are just things that happen to you. You must accept them. If a sorrowful event occurs, you naturally must feel sorrow, and all you can do is hope some happy event comes along very soon so you can feel better.

But here's a truth that you might not have been taught: Feelings are not just emotions that happen to you. Feelings are reactions you choose to have. You choose to be embarrassed by someone else. You choose to feel angry for reasons you can't explain. You choose to be depressed because of unfortunate events that have occurred that you did not ask for. These feelings, you believe, are just "who you are," and you've never thought you could do anything about them.

What if you had a different set of fundamental beliefs about who you are and how your life works? What if you went through life with the conviction that there is no problem that is all-encompassing? What if you believed that you are defined not by your problems, but by your attributes?

Everything you do in your life comes out of your core fundamental beliefs about who you are. All your attitudes that you present to others, and the way you behave in this world, are generated by what you believe. Let me give you a simple example. When someone cuts you off in traffic, what generally happens? You develop a sour attitude, don't you? You murmur curses about that person under your breath. You might go so far as to catch up with that person and cut him off. Why did such an angry emotion pop up in you? Because of your belief system! You believe that a person who would do something like that to you could only be an arrogant, dirty punk.

What, on the other hand, if you believed that such a person who would drive that way must be in a real hurry, perhaps has an emergency, and that the best thing to do would be to back off and give him some room? Then your entire attitude toward the situation would be different. Your day wouldn't be ruined by your own anger at that driver.

Let's say there are two identical twins. For some reason, one of these twins believes that she is ugly. Perhaps she had a bad experience or overheard a conversation that led her to feel that she was not attractive. One day, she is walking down the street and a group of boys all start to point, giggle, and laugh. What does she think?

That they are laughing at her. Why? Because she is ugly. How does this make her feel? Uglier. What will she do? Run. Cry. Hide.

Now, let's take her identical twin. For whatever reason, she believes that she is gorgeous, that she is God's gift to mankind. Whether she is really beautiful or not is immaterial. She believes that she's beautiful. One day, she too is walking down the street. A group of boys start to point, giggle, and laugh. What does she think? She thinks they are flirting with her. How does this make her feel? Great! What will she do? Strut!

What the two girls had was the exact same experience with two different results—and it was all because of their belief systems. In essence, by choosing what to believe, their emotions, attitudes, and behaviors were completely different.

I am convinced that we cannot permanently change our behavior over time unless we are first willing to change what we are willing to believe. Think about the beliefs you hold now. If you're like everyone else, then the majority of the beliefs you have come from sources outside yourself. As children you get your beliefs from your parents, teachers, and friends. As adults, you get them from your work, peers, and media. You have beliefs that are often based on misinterpretations of past experiences. And then, saddest of all, once you hold those beliefs as truth, you think they are unchangeable. You say to yourself and to others, "That's just who I am. That's the way I act. It's who I have always been."

Is that really the way you want to live? What an unfortunate belief it is to think, even for a moment, that you are somehow set up to lose—as though some of us have what it takes to win and some do not. What an unfortunate belief it is to think that you are destined to be the way you are, that you cannot overcome whatever problems lay before you. How misguided it is that so many of you believe that to overcome life's challenges, to be a great winner in life, you need to be someone lucky enough to have avoided life's pitfalls.

I'm sorry, but life just doesn't work that way—and deep down, you know it. You know people who were given all the best breaks in life but who still did nothing with their lives. You know genius "whiz kids" who never lived up to their potential, brilliant college graduates who have gotten buried in dead-end jobs and high school valedictorians voted "Most Likely to Succeed" who are never heard from again. And you no doubt know stories of people who didn't let formidable obstacles prevent them from making an impact in this world. Despite blindness and deafness, Helen Keller learned to read and write, graduated cum laude from Radcliffe in 1904, and became a brilliant author. Despite his deformities and dwarfism, Toulouse-Lautrec created exceptional paintings that made him one of the great talents of the Impressionist era. Despite a nervous system disorder that severely limited his speech and confined him to a wheelchair, Stephen Hawking did work in theoretical physics that stands as one of the most important contributions to understanding the universe.

These people could have spent their time complaining or feeling overwhelmed by their "problems." We would have understood if they had. But they thought through their predicaments, and they decided that their problems were not all-consuming. They realized they still had plenty to do with what they had. They defined themselves by their attributes, not by their setbacks. They were like those beautiful plants you often see growing up in the middle of an asphalt driveway—little twigs that are able to push their way up through a tough surface and survive against vicious odds.

You, too, can do the same thing. In the same way you learned to have self-defeating thoughts, you can learn not to have them. You can learn not to be unhappy, angry, hurt, or frustrated. You have the power to think whatever you choose to allow into your head. If something just "pops" into your head, you have the power to make it go away. You have the power to decide that a particular emotion is a "choice" rather than a condition of life. And you have the power, similarly, to choose beliefs that empower you, that bring out your best.

Not long after I told my doctors that I wasn't going to live my life with false hopelessness, I decided to escape from the hospital. Well, okay, I decided to sneak out for the evening. I enlisted my fiancée, Dallas, and my friend John in my plan. Waiting until after the dinner hour, Dallas, John, and I made our way to the already dark parking lot. We had made it appear as though they were simply taking me for a relaxing after-dinner stroll through the hospital; then we suddenly darted through a side door leading to freedom.

Of course, loading me into a car was not exactly easy. I was still wearing the halo brace, which kept me from bending my upper body, head, or neck. John's small Volkswagen presented quite a problem. It had those little doors, and I was a person who couldn't exactly bend. Using John's strength and Dallas's creativity, they pushed and pulled until I finally found myself in the front seat. It felt strange to be in a car again. It had been months since I had been away from the hospital. It was a cold evening, but I was dressed warmly.

John carefully and slowly drove the car down the street. Before long we pulled into the parking lot of a theater. We were going to the movies. It then occurred to me that to the other moviegoers, I must have looked like Frankenstein. John and Dallas had tried to cover up part of that halo brace with the hood of my sweatshirt. However, the bolts that came from the forehead area protruded out from the hood and the steel halo shone, even in the moonlight. The ticket taker had a hard time not revealing his thoughts as he stared at me. I looked like I was straight from some kind of torture chamber in a horror movie.

For many people, my image or condition was difficult to accept. They pitied me. They had trouble even looking at me. But at the movie theater, I smiled at the ticket taker and said, "Hey, how are you doing? You doing okay?" I had decided that I would choose my own reality and not let anyone else choose it for me.

People must have thought I was crazy that I decided to be happy. In fact, a few years ago, I was able to get ahold of all my medical records from that stay in the hospital. It included medications, doctors' notes, complications, and my case manager's recommendations. And it also finally gave me an answer to a question that had always bothered me about my time there. During much of my hospital stay, my doctor, the infamous Dr. Kelly, kept sending psychiatrists to see me. At one time, he had me separated from a room I shared with several other patients to my own room. I certainly wasn't complaining—I loved having my own room—but it did seem odd at the time. Right there, in the middle of this massive medical journal, I found the reason.

There was a report that said I was suffering from "excessive happiness." That's what it said. My medical condition was "excessive happiness." The doctors felt I laughed too much and was in too good of a mood much of the time.

The doctors noted in my record that they felt my state of "excessive happiness" was keeping me in a state of denial about my condition. They felt that the problem was exacerbated by (in his words) "a loving family." Their solution was to do several things:

1. *Keep me in psychiatric counseling;*
2. *Isolate me from other patients;*
3. *Limit my exposure to my family and friends.*

Excessive happiness! I never knew there was such a disorder. I didn't know you could be too happy.

Perhaps the good Dr. Kelly should have thought again about my attitude. When I decided that I would determine what I would believe, it was as if an indescribable sense of well-being washed over me. I realized that whatever pain or sorrow I had been given, there was something inside me strong enough to bear the weight of it. I realized that within myself was a stability that could never be taken away by other people.

Now I know there are some of you still thinking, "Okay, another Art Berg rah-rah talk." Look, I'm not saying that I never again had a bad day. I had to work at unlearning many of the negative thinking habits I had spent my life following. But despite my circumstances, I eventually became a truly changed person and eventually took my life to a place far beyond what even my wildest dreams used to be.

My attitude is not a rare gift handed only to the chosen few. You too can make that choice. It is there for those of you who want to create new worlds, and it is there for those of you who simply want to improve your daily lives. I don't care what position you're in right now. You can start changing virtually anything and everything about your life by making this choice to live in a framework of happiness, to refuse to let circumstances or conditions or other people determine your state of mind. With this tool, you will have the certainty that you can create the reality you want, that you can determine the experience of your own life, and that you can stay focused on the things in your life that matter most rather than the things that matter least. Instead of searching for shortcuts to make your life easier, you will start looking for challenges to make your life stronger. Instead of needing some outside motivation to get you over another hurdle, you will cherish the opportunity to hold yourself to the highest of life's standards. The inner drive you will develop will give you the power to live your life with a different level of quality, to implement change with more elegance and with far more effectiveness, and to find a tremendous joy in the process—a way of looking at the world that constantly increases your sense of appreciation and gratitude.

SEVEN

Courageous People Are Not Unafraid

After reading this chapter title, you're probably saying, "Sorry, Art. This isn't me. I'm hardly someone who is afraid. And I'm certainly not scared of change. Otherwise, why would I have bought your book?"

Well, it's easy to read a book. It's hard to make real change. And the reason it's hard to make change is because you're full of fear. I'm not exaggerating. The common thread I have found among people who seem emotionally or professionally paralyzed, people who seem unable to pull themselves out of their ruts, is fear. They are afraid of the idea of change—any change. They talk about making changes, they gravitate to the idea of change, yet they ultimately fear losing what is familiar. They are afraid of killing off their old identities and their old securities—no matter how poorly those identities and securities have benefited them in the past—and making the decision to fly adventurously into the unknown.

In the business world, for instance, I have had meetings with human resources executives who explain to me their "unique set of problems." Chief executive officers have described for me how they are plagued by "new" competitive challenges that are a "first" in their industry. Managers tell me that no other business has the kind of "unrealistic expectations and limited resources" that theirs do.

What's really going on here? These people are afraid. They are driven by fear.

I also meet people who talk to me about their personal lives. They tell me about the problems in their families that seem "unfixable." They tell me about their "conflicts" regarding whether to begin or end a relationship, whether to change jobs, or whether to go back to school. They tell me they "don't know what to do" regarding their own or their loved one's illness. They tell me they are "anxious" over retirement, over getting old, over making mistakes, over losing weight.

What's really going on here? These people are afraid. They are driven by fear.

If you think you are not in some way driven by fear, then you need to think again. Fear works on us at many different levels. We have external fear, which is the fear of things happening over which we have no control (i.e., losing our spouse or going bankrupt), and we have internal fear, which is the fear of losing our inner sense of pride or status or confidence that comes from such events as the loss of a spouse or bankruptcy. We fear feeling lonely, feeling vulnerable, feeling that our lives might be out of control. We fear rejection, we fear failure, we fear dealing with our own pain. We fear losing our feelings of security.

There is nothing more crippling—and I mean that literally—than fear. Fear produces something like an astigmatism of the intellect. Fear is very, very real. Fear is what closes your mouth when you want to speak. It wears down your physical vitality and can actually make you sick. When you are driven by fear, you are simply not aware of what your options are. When you are trapped in fear, you tend not to see how a problem can be turned around. You let your fear grow into a monster that fills you with doubts and excuses. Your fear is like self-fulfilling pessimism: It tends to create situations that justify fearing.

In fact, fear is the main factor that stops so many of you from capitalizing on opportunities. It is what keeps you from making any significant improvement in your life. It is what makes you live your life through the expectations of others rather than listen to your heart and pursue a vision of yourself for which you have real passion. It is fear that has made you decide that it is still best to live reactively from day to day, sheltering yourselves, staying paralyzed.

As a result, you spend more time trying to avoid life's challenges than facing them. You know that transforming your life can produce anxiety, and because anxiety frightens you, you back off altogether. Even if you find yourself thrown by life into horrible circumstances, it's still scary to begin the process of changing to get out of those circumstances.

I don't paint a pretty picture, do I? But be honest with yourself. If you lived a life that was not driven by fear, would you spend another moment procrastinating? Would you do something more than idly hope that your problems will just one day disappear?

Would you ever rely on excuses to justify the problems facing you, using the language of psychology to categorize yourself as someone who can't get better? Would you ever say to yourself, "Wait a second, these difficulties that have come my way are just too big to handle?"

There's no other way around it. If you're going to take charge of your life, if you're ever going to obtain real fulfillment, then you have to confront your fear. If you ever want to get away from the boring, sheltered shore to venture out to the daring seas beyond, to find real satisfaction, accomplish more in your career, and do the most good for other people, then you have to get over your fear.

And how do you get over your fear? Because this is such an important subject, I'm going to talk about fear in other places throughout the book, but for now, here's the lesson I want you to learn:

It's okay to be afraid.

Does that sound elementary? Hardly. When a major crisis confronts you, or when the time has come for you to step up and make significant changes in your life, you don't need to wait for some superhuman dose of courage. You don't need to wait until you feel fearless. I don't think there is such a thing, except in comic books and bad Hollywood action movies, as a fearless person.

As a matter of fact, I like to think of courage as nothing more than recognizing that you are fearful about something and doing it anyway. Instead of running from fear, which only makes the fear bigger, a courageous person takes some sort of action. Instead of staying in one place until he or she no longer feels fear, a courageous person decides to push forward, to keep moving, to act in spite of that fear.

I see people reading books all the time on how to beat back their fears, and I want to stop and tell them, "You don't need a book. You just need to go do whatever it is that scares you." Don't waste time analyzing why you are afraid or the factors that add up to fear. Just take action. As Ralph Waldo Emerson once wrote, "Do the thing you fear and the death of fear is certain."

Let me take you back to my days at the Santa Clara Valley Medical Center in California. Strangely enough, one of the things that filled me with fear was eating meals. Don't take this wrong. Eating itself wasn't what was creating the fear. In reality, I was afraid of becoming dependent on other people. I was afraid of becoming comfortable with physical dependence for all of life's necessities. I also had fear on another level. I was afraid of looking ridiculous as I tried to relearn even the simplest of tasks. I was afraid to fail. So, eating wasn't it, even though the old, familiar task had suddenly become very intimidating. It caused huge anxiety, because I knew if I couldn't feed myself, which I wasn't able to do in those first months, then I was going to have a very difficult, if not impossible, time handling other tasks.

It wasn't the food that was the problem. It was getting the food into my mouth that was the challenge. Because my hands were paralyzed, I had to use a special instrument to help me pick up my fork and raise it. To complicate matters, I had no functioning stomach muscles to help keep me upright and no use of my neck and head to assist in keeping me balanced. Adding to the problem was that my halo brace caused me to be extremely top-heavy. I was required to wear a chest strap to keep me from falling out of my chair.

As a result, the hospital assigned a physical therapist to feed me each day. Never had I felt so helpless. For my own sense of self-esteem, I knew I had to learn to eat by myself, but I was also scared of trying it. If I failed, I would be humiliated, and that would lead, of course, to even greater fear.

But one day, I realized that if I risked nothing, I was risking even more. I was staying right where I was. So one morning, I told the therapist that I wanted to eat breakfast by myself. Not only that, I said, I wanted to eat breakfast without having to wear the restraining belt around my chest.

The therapist responded, "Are you absolutely sure?" Putting on what I hoped appeared to be a confident smile, I assured her of my desire. Hesitantly, she unfastened the strap and left.

I vividly remember what I was going to eat that morning. It was scrambled eggs with a hot biscuit. Reaching for the fork, I maneuvered it between my fingers to try and get some kind of a hold on it. Once it felt reasonably secure, I lifted it toward the plate. But with my arm extended directly in front of me, I was presented with a balance problem I had not anticipated. Even though my sense of equilibrium was not completely accurate, I recognized from the sight of the fast approaching plate of food that I was falling forward. Having little use of my weak arms, any attempt to stop myself was futile. With the weight of the halo brace pushing me forward, my face landed squarely in my plate of food.

I listened for a moment to see if I could hear anyone. Then, using my weakened arms, I tried to sit myself up again. That option was out. I was stuck right there, facedown in my scrambled eggs. Now, with a whole new perspective on the four basic food groups, two thoughts crossed my mind. The first was that this was probably going to be one of the longest twenty-eight minutes of my life. The second thought was that I probably wouldn't get into a more advantageous position for eating for a long time. So I ate my breakfast! I've never had the same appreciation for scrambled eggs and biscuits since.

After exactly thirty minutes, the therapist walked back into the room and, seeing my situation, she quickly rushed to my side and pulled me out of my plate. I showed obvious relief to have my vision of the room restored. The therapist, noticing that the plate was shiny and clean, excitedly asked me, "Well, how did you do?"

"All right," I responded, "It was a little tough getting the butter on the biscuit, but I did okay!"

You'll notice that I didn't exactly succeed in my task. But I felt jubilant. I began to develop a greater self-confidence not because I ate breakfast like I was supposed to, but because I actually confronted the situation before me.

It is always better to fight fear than to live with a feeling of helplessness. Why? What you'll realize is that the fight itself is far less frightening than living with the numbing sense of dread that comes from doing nothing. When we transform fear into a companion—not an anchor that holds us in one spot—then we transform our lives. When we realize that the issue is not the fear itself, but how we treat the fear, then we can take a major step toward getting rid of the emotional paralysis in our lives.

It's like learning to snow ski. If you've ever tried to do it, then you know that to ski, you have to learn to lean forward and feel like you're falling downhill. To be a good skier, you have to lean past what is called the "fall line." The problem is that most of us have spent our lives trying not to fall. It's our impulse to fight against gravity. As a result, when we're on a hill learning to snow ski, we naturally lean back into the hill—which makes us terrible skiers. Only when we "act out" our fear— when we go with gravity and ski in a way that makes us think we're going to fall—do we realize we will not fall at all! We actually flow down the hill without resistance.

One of the reasons Outward Bound programs are so popular with business executives is that people come back realizing that even small attempts to confront their fears and take risks do wonders for their self-perception. In these programs, they are alone in the wilderness, or they try to climb a huge mountain, or they raft down a wild river. Even if they are not 100 percent successful in achieving their goal, they feel wondrously alive from the risks they have taken. Their adrenaline races and their hearts beat faster. They know that by immersing themselves in their fears, they have touched a great, vibrant power deep inside them. And when they go back to their real lives, they now know that fear is not bad. It can be the source of tremendous energy and exhilaration. By taking a risk in one area, they become more confident about taking a risk in another.

One great technique to deal with your fears in the face of adversity is to recount past challenges that you have successfully overcome. Your ability to manage present circumstances is improved when you recall past fears that were never ultimately realized.

Every one of you, I'm sure, has an experience from the past where you applied faith, persistence, creativity, and hard work to better your circumstances. Granted, whatever you faced in your past might not be as dramatic as your present circumstances. When I broke my neck and lay paralyzed in a hospital bed, I certainly had nothing as devastating from my history to build on. But I did have past moments when I had struggled with feelings of despair, loss, hopelessness, and a fear that things would never change.

I was taken back to a time when I was seventeen years old and struggling socially and academically. Throughout my youth, I had made many poor choices. I was not a juvenile delinquent by any stretch of the imagination. I didn't smoke or drink. But I tended to resist authority. I never liked people, especially teachers, telling me what to do. By high school I was cutting classes and sneaking off to the bowling alley or to the miniature golf course. I was also getting into a lot of fights. I was small as a kid, and other kids thought they could pick on me. My feelings of inadequacy often led me to physically lash out at others. I lost most of the fights, but I still kept fighting.

Things began to go downhill my junior year. Although I had an IQ of 142 and was an avid reader, I was failing four classes. Because I kept getting into fights, I was suspended from high school more than once and finally kicked out. I'll never forget the vice principal telling me that I was a complete loser who would never do anything with his life. Separated from my friends, attending a neighboring high school, I hit an emotional low in those next weeks. I started goofing off in class, becoming even more disruptive.

It was then that I began to sense a hopeless feeling. I told my mother I felt like I was drowning. I was spiraling downward and I couldn't seem to hold on. At one point, sitting in my room because I was grounded, the thought occurred to me, "What if I just ended it now? I'm a failure, I'm a screw-up, everyone thinks I'm worthless. Who would care if I died?"

The thought scared me so much that I knelt beside my bed that night and cried out to God—the deepest, most soulful outburst I had ever made. I told God that I was at the bottom, that the whole world had rejected me, and what I needed to know was whether He knew I existed, was I important to Him, and did it matter to Him that I was hurting.

Later that night, a feeling came over me—just a small one, not anything dramatic in a biblical way—and I realized that I was not alone, that I knew I was loved, and that I would get through whatever problems I was facing. A few days later, my father gave me a cassette tape by the world-renowned motivational speaker Zig Ziglar titled *Biscuits, Fleas and Pump Handles*. I listened to it many times over the course of the next few weeks. I might have listened to it 100 times. My attitude slowly began to improve. My thoughts began to evolve and change in small increments. Soon I came to the realization that my problems were never too overwhelming for me to give up the idea of happiness.

My circumstances did not change overnight, of course. With each passing day, I had to work to improve my life. But over a period of time, my grades improved, my teachers respected me, my parents trusted me, my friends believed in me, my old high school welcomed me back, and life was good again.

Is a struggling teenage identity crisis the same as a tragic car accident? No, but if you think about it, the feelings I experienced in both were similar. By looking back over time, I realized that none of my fears were ever realized, and that I was far more resilient than I imagined.

So even if the road before you right now seems uncomfortable and a little scary, don't worry. Fear will be a constant in your life. In fact, the fear might never leave you. But it is not the absence of fear that will make you confident about your ability to change. As I learned after my accident, change is possible despite even the most extreme level of fear. And each time you act in spite of your fear, you discover even greater, deeper courage.

EIGHT

Start Sweating the Small Stuff

STRATEGY: IF YOU WANT TO MAKE BIG
CHANGES IN YOUR LIFE, DON'T FORGET
TO MAKE THE SMALL ONES

A philosopher once said that the most difficult problem in life was getting out of a warm bed into a cold room. He had a point. The longer you lie there and think how unpleasant it will be to get up, the more difficult it becomes. To put it another way: people who get things done in this world don't wait for the spirit to move them. They move the spirit.

Have you ever watched good salespeople? They know that the hardest sales call to make is the first one of the day. It is so easy to procrastinate, to drink a second cup of coffee, to flip through the newspaper. What the best salespeople learn is that the only way to start is to start. Don't deliberate. Don't postpone getting started.

Just pick up the phone or show up at someone's office and say "Good morning" and make your presentation.

And that's what it takes for real change to happen for you. I am convinced a lot of you have forgotten what changing your life really means. You lock onto the ideas we discussed in the previous section about getting the right attitude, and then you think your work is done. Or others of you do go ahead and make a couple of initial big steps, feel some sense of change working in your life, and then you think your work is done, too. You've gotten the ball rolling, you say. Now everything will take care of itself.

Please, look at that ball again. I can bet you that it's already stopped rolling.

As I have said many times in this book, life's struggles never come to an end. You cannot make one big effort to change your life and then be done. Because life is a constant struggle, change, too, must be a constant in your life. You must strive ceaselessly to improve yourself, to condition your mind, to develop your skills, and to always move forward. Isaac Newton put it this way: "A body at rest stays at rest until a force acts on it." You have to be that force. A constant force. Otherwise, you stop moving forward.

There are many of you who believe you can't take action until you get all of your "ducks in a row." You are going to get started on your new life, you tell yourself, just as soon as you read that new book on accounting, or lose that extra ten pounds, or save some more money, or get the kids back in school for the year, or get better organized. The list can go on and on. For whatever reason, something always needs to happen before you can take action. Your excuses always sound reasonable and even logical, but all the excuses do is prevent you from ever realizing your goals and dreams. Isn't it interesting that those of you always waiting to get your "ducks in a row" before you take any sizable, measurable action usually end up with just a lot of dead ducks!

Or there are some of you who think you are "getting started" on your problems by doing other things. Have you ever looked at your "to do" list for the day and immediately attacked the easiest ones because then you could "check them off?" This only gives you a false sense of accomplishment. Human nature is to avoid the difficult. The tendency for many of us is to leave the most important tasks until a "better time of the day." Unfortunately, better times of the day rarely come.

And then there are those of you who think you aren't making changes unless you're making big, earth-shattering changes. Wrong again. Regardless of where we are in life, we can make significant changes by initially taking very small risks, and then moving to larger ones. In other words, one step leads to the next, which leads to the next and then to the next one after that. Don't forget that the little changes are just as important as the big ones. Or to put it another way: Don't forget to sweat the small stuff.

I have found several strategies to get beyond procrastination and make yourself "just do it." The first is, when you get up in the morning and review your schedule for the day, ask yourself several questions to help you focus on what's most valuable and important, regardless of your reluctance to get started:

1. *What are you avoiding today?*
2. *If you could only accomplish one thing, what would make the biggest impact on your life and career?*
3. *What is preventing you from starting right now?*

The second idea is the willingness to begin now, regardless of whether I have a road map. People think they need a ten-point plan to know exactly where to go and how to get there. Notice that this book doesn't have any ten-point anything. Real change doesn't work that way. You have to have courage to get started now, even though you aren't completely sure how you will finish. You must have the faith to begin going down a road even though you may not have a detailed, completed map.

And the third idea is to remind yourself that your changes don't always have to be great ones. I will never forget during those first days and weeks after my accident how weak and thin my body became. Before the accident, I had weighed as much as 168 pounds, standing six feet tall. Within a very short period of time, I had lost forty-eight pounds. With those pounds, I also lost much of my physical strength—even in the few muscles that continued to work. My days and hours at the hospital became filled with relearning the essentials of life. I was like a child starting all over again.

Each morning a therapist would come to my bedside and stretch my legs, arms, and hands to keep them as limber as possible. Sometimes it was frustrating and discouraging. I felt foolish for not being able to do even the simplest things. At one time a therapist had me practicing for an hour each day stacking children's building blocks. You know the ones—they have letters on the sides with pictures of ducks and lambs. The exercise was to improve my hand dexterity and to teach me to pick up small objects again. Hour after hour I struggled to make my hands and arms useful and productive again. At times I sat and stared at the hands that once did so much so easily. Now they labored over the weight and challenge of picking up a tiny building block from a table.

Later, I tried to hold a felt-tip pen between my stiff fingers and make marks on a piece of paper. After hours and days of effort, I began to form those marks into letters and words and then sentences. Each day, for an hour, I would struggle to write thank-you notes and brief letters. Each letter was barely legible. Before my accident, I had beautiful, flowing handwriting. Now I had the handwriting of a 100-year-old man. A short note took as long as an hour or two, even though it consisted of only four or five sentences.

Then finger splints were made for me so I could learn to type again. From typing sixty words per minute, I had to slowly peck out each letter with exacting effort and deliberation. During other parts of the day, I spent time lying on large mats that were raised about eighteen inches off the floor. Under the direction of a therapist, I was being taught how to roll over again. I know that sounds silly, but these are just examples of the things that I relearned through hours of work and practice. They also taught me to get up on my elbows and try to drag my body from one end of the mat to the other. It didn't do much good. I could barely move my body at all.

Sometimes it was difficult to see any long-term advantage that could come from my struggles. I questioned the therapist, asking why I needed to learn to drag myself around a mat. She thought for a moment, then with a smile on her face that showed a sense of pride in her well-thought-out answer, she said, "In case there is a fire at night, you can roll out of bed onto the floor and drag yourself to safety."

Sounded good, but I had one more question: "How do I get the door open once I drag myself all the way across the room?" That ended that therapy class for the day.

Let me describe my least favorite part of therapy. I would be put on the infamous tilt table—a padded table with straps at the head and foot. In efforts to keep my blood pressure and circulation functioning properly, it was important that I use the tilt table daily. While laying on my back, my knees and chest would be strapped down. Then, with a therapist at the controls, I would be hydraulically tilted on the table until I was slightly inclined. I breathed heavily from the need for oxygen. I focused as much as I could on objects across the room. Before I knew it the objects were becoming fuzzy and unclear. Black spots began to appear and my head started to throb. I tried to breathe again, but I felt I was drifting away. The edges of my vision became dark. Eventually I would lose all oxygen-carrying blood to the brain, and the room would go black.

I had no sensation of where I was, where I had been, or how long I had been gone. Then I would be lowered, brought back to reality, and then raised again. I could hear voices again. My normal breathing returned, and even though my head was splitting wide open with a headache, I could see the lights of the ceiling clearly.

This was done every day for weeks, the table being tilted farther back each time, as the therapists tried to build my endurance to a point where I could maintain a standing position. That feeling of passing out was something I never quite got used to, although I certainly became familiar with the aspirin bottle.

Later, after I had been in the hospital for a while, I was challenged with even more creative means of adapting to life's new circumstances. Believe it or not, they brought me to the kitchen. This is what they called occupational therapy, although I had a difficult time imagining anyone hiring me as a cook. They began by having me create a simple peanut butter sandwich. I say "create," because that's the best word to describe what it looked like after I was done trying to get the peanut butter off the knife and onto the bread. "Scrambled sandwich" would have been more appropriate. However, I swallowed my pride, along with the sandwich, to prove my self-reliance.

Then came the fun part. They actually wanted me to bake a cake. I said, "No problem." I began by tearing off the top of the cake mix box with my teeth. Luckily, I got at least half of the mix into the bowl. The therapist just watched and smiled. I was glad to see that at least she was enjoying this. Then came the eggs. How does a guy with limited use of his hands and arms gently crack an egg into a bowl without getting bits of shell into the mix? I thought for a moment. A smile spread across my face. I gently cradled the egg in the palm of my hand, raised it above the bowl, and slammed it into the mix! It broke, all right! Egg and mix went everywhere—all over me, the table, and even the therapist. I think she lost all hope of me becoming a cook. By the way, the cake was delicious, as long as you watched out for those little white shells.

If you're thinking that I wasn't exactly making historic progress in those early days at the hospital, you're right. My initial accomplishments were not particularly noteworthy. But I was at least taking some action—and that's all that mattered. Some of the greatest miracles of my life have not come about by grand events, but rather by the little things I have chosen to do every day. Very often it is the little things that make the biggest difference. It is the little, thoughtful things we say to a spouse or child. It is the relationships we build by little acts of trust and caring over the years. It is our daily rituals of health, diet, and exercise that determine our ultimate health, not some thirty-day all-protein diet. It is what we read and study every day that stays with us for the long term, while the subject matters that we crammed for are forgotten shortly after the test is done. It is our small, quiet moments of prayer and solace that determine the depth of our faith, not our desperate pleadings when our life is in the balance. I have found that during those moments of my life when I have felt the most lost, it is because I had been ignoring many of the "little things" for too long.

I was setting a new tone for my life. And that's what you can do yourself. Don't make the mistake of doing nothing. Standing still is not an acceptable option. You can be like a deer on the highway caught in the headlights—freezing in your tracks until life passes you by—or you can move. If you move, you increase the odds of living longer and better.

Even if all the changes don't work the way you hope, you are doing wonders for yourself just by actively engaging in change. Every time you confront the stagnant areas in your life that you previously have avoided, you will find that your fears are lessening and your confidence is growing. And with the increased confidence, you will want to change even more—to get out of your old patterns and start daring to do the things that have caused you the most emotional terror in the past. You will find yourself filled with an energy you haven't had before to pursue your own goals.

NINE

❋

The Problem Isn't What You Can't Do,
It's What You Don't Do

STRATEGY: EVEN WHEN CERTAIN CHANGE IS IMPOSSIBLE,
YOU CAN STILL MAKE CHANGES

I'm always a little amused when I hear someone say that infamous old self-help phrase, "What the mind can conceive, it can achieve."

The truth is, you cannot achieve anything you conceive. If you're not tall and don't have certain athletic gifts, there are no changes you can make that will turn you into an NBA basketball player. You will not be the world's greatest salesman if the product you are selling is terrible.

Obviously, after my wreck, there were some things I simply could not change, the biggest of which is that I would not be able to walk again. Becoming a quadriplegic meant that I had limited functions in all four extremities of my body. (If I had limited functions in just the lower half of my body, I would have been a paraplegic.) The damage in your body all depends on which vertebrae you break. I broke the fifth vertebra from the top. Christopher Reeve broke the first and the second. That's why his disability is different from mine. That's why he can't shrug his shoulders or continue to breathe completely on his own for long periods of time without a respirator.

Because I had lost all functional use of the right triceps—the muscle that makes the arm go up and down—my right arm just sat there. And I had no use of my hands. None of my fingers moved independently, which made it just a little difficult to communicate, especially when I was in a car and wanted to make an angry gesture at a bad driver.

But even though I could not change the fact that my hands wouldn't work, I realized I could adapt to my condition in such a way to make my hands useful. I'll show you. Put your hands up in the air, would you please? Make your fingers and your wrists go limp. Keep your fingers loose, and bring your wrists back up. Notice that your thumb and your index finger come closer together. When you flap your hands down, the thumb and index finger go farther apart, and when you flap your hands back up, the thumb and index finger come closer together. Aside from the fact that you may look somewhat ridiculous, what you're doing is a medical term called tenodesis. All it means is that you don't need the individual independent use of your fingers in order to get some function from your hands. You can use the tendons in your forearm. Just drawing your wrist back will pinch your fingers in close enough together that with a whole lot of practice you can learn to pick up a fork, shake someone's hand, write, and do many of the essential functions of life. Which is exactly what I learned to do.

After I mastered that, I continued to think about what else I could do to improve the use of my hands. I could have stopped there and said, "Well, I feel pretty satisfied at the changes I made." But, in fact, I wasn't satisfied. As a quadriplegic, I experience muscle spasms. All that means is that the paralyzed muscles in my body still tend to fire from time to time, just not always voluntarily. The muscles in my legs can jump suddenly. The muscles in the small of my back can jerk me backward. It happens to almost all quadriplegics, and it can be very painful. Many quadriplegics will take a variety of prescription drugs in order to alleviate the discomfort and avoid some of the risk. Because of the strength of many of those drugs, the drugs often leave you feeling groggy and lightheaded. So I chose not to take them. I decided to take this "problem" of muscle spasms and try to turn it to my advantage. I began working at getting my hands to spasm when I wanted them to. Eventually, I could get my hands to open and close automatically without moving my wrist. That seemingly small, imperceptible function enabled me to do a number of things I otherwise could not have done. It enabled me to turn a doorknob, open a jar of peanut butter, and shake hands in such a way that you actually think I have a grip. As I got better at controlling my muscle spasms, I could even pick things up off the floor.

What I did was focus on what I had and not on what I didn't have. Through that focus, I was able to make more changes.

So what does that story have to do with your own journey? It means there is always something you can do to adapt to anything that comes your way. Those individuals who are the most indispensable in this disposable world are those who are the most willing to adapt. It's a willingness to rework what you do and how you do it in the process of moving forward. And it means not being limited to just a narrow focus of how to do things.

In fact, when you're trying to change, it is sometimes prefer-able not to rely so much on your experience. In today's world of change, that experience is almost a negative. Why? Because expe-rience can tie you to the past. Experience ties you to old ways of doing things and old ways of thinking that for today may no longer be nearly as effective. For more effective change, you need flexi-bility—a willingness to listen more to others than to yourself and to try new things rather than repeat what you've always done.

It is human nature, of course, to focus on what we used to pos-sess, what we don't now possess, and what someone else has that we don't. But experience has taught me that if I focus predomi-nantly on what I do not have, I am very seldom productive. More often than not, I am frustrated and discouraged. But if I focus only on what I have to work with, I start finding new solutions to old problems.

Ultimately, the willingness to keep changing is the key to find-ing all the best qualities within yourself. Those of you in business know what I'm talking about. If you remain rigid and inflexible in the twenty-first-century marketplace, you will be less valuable to the marketplace and eventually out of a job. I once spoke to a company that had manufacturing lead times of two weeks, which at that time was the leader in that particular industry. However, the executive team felt that if they got comfortable with two weeks, eventually someone else would come along and unseat them as the industry front-runners. So the executive team imple-mented new changes to incorporate what they called a "lean man-ufacturing" strategy. Almost immediately, because the changes were hard to implement, the lead times soared to six weeks, then to eight weeks. The company was becoming the laughingstock of the industry. But then the changes began to take effect. The tide began to turn back to four weeks. Then three. Then finally two.

Today, the company has a manufacturing lead time of one week, and no one else can touch them.

Just as a good chief executive officer keeps looking for ways to change because he or she knows that nothing will be the same in five years, so you, too, as the chief executive officer of your own life, must always be looking for better ways to make changes. You must be flexible enough to get around the new obstacles that are looming on the horizon, and you must be willing to change course if you have to. I will never forget the story told by Frank Koch in *Proceedings,* the magazine of the Naval Institute:

Two battleships assigned to the training squadron had been at sea on maneuvers in heavy weather for several days. I was serving on the lead battleship and was on watch on the bridge as night fell. The visibility was poor with patchy fog, so the captain remained on the bridge keeping an eye on all activities. Shortly after dark, the lookout on the wing of the bridge reported, "Light, bearing on the starboard bow."

"Is it steady or moving astern?" the captain called out. The lookout replied, "Steady, captain," which meant we were on a dangerous collision course with that ship.

The captain then called to the signalman, "Signal that ship: We are on a collision course, advise you change course 20 degrees." Back came the signal, "Advisable for you to change course 20 degrees." The captain said, "I'm a captain, change course 20 degrees."

"I'm a seaman second class," came the reply. "You had better change course 20 degrees."

By that time the captain was furious. He spat out, "I'm a battleship. Change course 20 degrees."

Back came the flashing light, "I'm a lighthouse."

We changed course.

Once you make the decision to keep fighting for change, the range of possibilities for discovering who you are can be are endless. By experimenting with new ways of doing things, you will eventually discover your full potential. By enduring your anxiety and consistently risking your best effort, you will achieve more than you ever believed possible. No, you won't be able to change everything. But you will have realized that you have spent far too long holding back your own potential.

Let me tell you one last story about my stay in the California hospital. I was using a heavy and cumbersome Everest-Jennings manual wheelchair. It's largely chrome, and weighs about sixty-five pounds. I felt clumsy and awkward in it. Maneuvering that big Everest-Jennings was difficult and tiresome at best, and it seemed evident to my therapist and doctor that an electric wheelchair would be a necessity for the rest of my life.

No one would have said a word if I had relented and given in to the electric wheelchair. No one would have said, "Art, you're not living up to your potential if you don't keep trying to change." But every time I made a small breakthrough, I kept asking myself, "What else can I change? What else can I do to expand the parameters of my potential?" I knew that if I got used to the ease and convenience of just pushing a button for my desires, my strength and my self-esteem would slowly deteriorate. So with each struggle in the old manual wheelchair came added strength and resolve. Each labored push produced a greater will to achieve and overcome.

I told the hospital staff that I was not going to leave that hospital in an electrical wheelchair. There had been a flood of new manual chairs coming into the marketplace that had been described as ultra-light and sporty, and that's what I said I needed. "You must use an electric wheelchair, Art," the nurses and therapists replied. "To get around this hospital on smooth linoleum floors is one thing, but for you to challenge the world without the use of a motor is not very feasible."

"You don't understand," I replied. "I do not want an electric wheelchair. I won't use it. I want a manual chair."

Finally, they consented to consider my proposal if I could pass a test of strength and ability. On the first floor of the hospital, a track had been laid out measuring one-eighth of a mile. If I could push that distance in less than thirty minutes, I could have my manual wheelchair. Dallas pushed me around the track the first time to give me a feel for what I had to do. There were few obstacles, just distance, so I felt confident I could meet the challenge.

With her stopwatch set, the therapist yelled, "Go!" Slowly, I crawled off the starting line. The first long hallway was a breeze. With Dallas walking at my side encouraging me, I felt that the rest of the track would be easily accomplished in the desired time limit. Rounding the first corner into the second long corridor, I felt the first real signs of fatigue. My arms began to feel like lead and my shoulders were sore. My slow pace slipped to less than a crawl. Each push seemed to take increasing amounts of energy and effort. I couldn't believe it. I had most of the distance left to go and already I was exhausted.

Biting my lower lip, I pushed on. My arms and shoulders were cramping, but somehow I managed to keep pushing. I rounded the second corner, and then the third. Completing the fourth corner, my final objective was in view—the finish line.

I could see the therapist smiling as I struggled to act as though I wasn't tired at all. I lifted my head and smoothly pushed across the line. The official time: twenty-eight minutes. I had made it.

You will have a similar moment when you can take an easier way—your version of the electric chair—or you can take the more difficult route. Imagine that you are now at a crossroads in your life. You must choose between two equally compelling directions.

There are two signs facing you, with arrows pointing toward different paths. One reads, "COMFORTABLE ROAD AHEAD. NO CHANGE REQUIRED." The arrow points down a familiar path that you have taken many times. While you may hate that road and even despise yourself for following it, you have been traveling there for so long that you know the way.

The other sign at the crossroads reads, "UNCOMFORTABLE ROAD AHEAD. CHANGE REQUIRED." It points to an unfamiliar path—and a new behavior for you. Going this way might cause some greater anxiety at first, but it could be the most productive route for you to take.

What shall it be? The easy path? Or the road less traveled? Ask yourself: Can you afford to maintain your unmoving place in life? Are you willing to stay in the status quo, or do you want to do something so that one day you will not look back on a life strewn with regrets?

As we struggle under the weight of our circumstances when the vision of our hopes and dreams grows dim, we must never forget what Robert Frost wrote about the positive impact that taking a less-traveled direction can make on a person's life:

> Two roads diverged in a wood and I—
> I took the one less traveled by.
> And that has made all the difference.

TEN

Learn to Fail Faster

Not long ago, when I was being interviewed on a television show, the host commented, "Art, you've had an unusual amount of success for such a young age. What would you attribute it to?"

"I've had an unusual amount of failure," I said.

So many of us are afraid to fail. We are conditioned to view failure as disgraceful. The idea is pounded into us early in our lives not to fail, not to lose. Our distorted interpretation of winners versus losers goes back to the famous Vince Lombardi quote, "Winning isn't everything, but wanting to win is." If we do fail, or if we have trouble recovering from a significant setback, we are instantly stigmatized, branded losers by a society that worships the bottom line. We feel ashamed, humiliated, ostracized by our friends and family. We feel profoundly isolated by what we perceive as our failures. Although we keep up a good front, assuring our families and the rest of the world that we are fine, we feel tormented by the realm of failure.

If you think about it, the Scarlet Letter in our society is "F." Contemplating someone else's failure can make us squirm with discomfort, or exhale in relief that it wasn't us who failed. And if we do happen to fail, we don't talk about failure to anyone else. It's fascinating to me how there are plenty of books on the nature of success but very few on the nature of failure.

How did this happen? For children, failure is a part of everyday life. While learning to walk, toddlers fail much more than they succeed—and we as parents understand and accept the process as an integral part of their learning. However, we don't apply the same principle to our own adult lives. We are very intolerant of our own failures. We often live in such a way as to avoid failure more than we live in a way to find success. It's like someone who wants to quit smoking, who is aware of the risks smokers face, but who won't try to quit because he knows that the majority of smoking cessation programs fail with a majority of smokers. So he keeps on reading the latest books and articles on the subject, telling himself that he will quit once the perfect program is developed.

What has happened to that person? You got it. He's become paralyzed. And until he changes his perspective of what failure means, he will remain paralyzed. His potential for success will always be limited.

The concept of failure is vastly underrated. Failure is simply a result of one particular action. It is never a condition that defines who you are—until you give up. The only time failure matters is when you stop making an effort, when you quit trying to achieve.

Yet so many of us are scared of looking like people in those old cartoons who keep trying to fix things but keep screwing up. Like the cartoon of the man painting himself into a corner of his living room. Or the one of the man building a boat in his cellar with no plan for getting it into the water. Or the one of the man who climbs out on a limb and begins to saw, blissfully unaware of what's about to happen to him.

Let me offer a starkly different view of those cartoons. Instead of really making a mess of things, those people are teaching themselves what it takes to be successful. As incompetent as they are—and okay, I admit, they look really incompetent—at least they are learning what not to do next time. They are willing to be a little embarrassed in order to reach a higher level of success.

Here's an example we can all relate to—losing weight. If you try to lose ten pounds and you don't, have you failed? No. The only thing that happened was that the attempt you made didn't work that time around. You didn't get the result you wanted. So you make another attempt, trying something else, and then you see if you get the result you want. If you don't, you try again another way. You're not failing. You're going through experiences to figure out how to get the results you want. It's exactly what scientists do in their laboratory. They are never discouraged by an experiment that fails, because it teaches them what to do, or what not to do, for their next experiment.

Major league baseball players understand that failure is an inescapable fact of their lives. They know that when they come to the plate, they are going to swing and miss more often than they swing and hit. Even the best hitter who ever lived—Ted Williams—failed at his task roughly seven out of every ten times he came to bat. He only got a hit about one-third of the time; the other two thirds of the time, he made an out. Yet Williams didn't avoid coming to the plate. He didn't avoid swinging. Instead of trying to hide from failure, he kept swinging. He accepted his failures at the plate and didn't make excuses. Instead, he dwelled on the hits.

Imagine if you knew you were going to fail two out of three times at something you tried. Wouldn't you feel like a failure? Wouldn't you think you were doing something terribly wrong? Wouldn't you want to give up? Wouldn't you spend a lot of time coming up with excuse after excuse to justify your "failure"?

As long as you remain afraid of failure—as long as you play the game of life hoping to avoid failure instead of trying to win—you will never find happiness. In fact, in today's world of unprecedented change, the best chance you have for success is to learn to fail faster. That's not a misprint. You need to fail faster. Try things, learn quickly from them if they don't work, correct them quickly, and move on. While others lament their own mistakes—which does nothing for them except slow down their lives—you are already at work "failing" again, reaching another milestone in your education. When you view each "failure" as nothing more than a temporary result, then you realize nothing you've done is final.

While I was growing up, my father, who worked for IBM for twenty-three years, shared with me a story that was often retold among IBM's management ranks. It was about a young executive who went straight from college to IBM and was given great responsibilities and important clients. Of course, with such an opportunity for great success came the equivalent opportunity for great mistakes. Soon the young executive made a decision that cost IBM more than five million dollars. The next day the president of IBM invited this young executive into his office for a chat. The young man walked into the president's office terrified that he had jeopardized his career in one risky decision. But during the nearly one-hour visit, the president said nothing about the financial loss IBM had just incurred. They just chatted about IBM. Finally, as the president stood to shake the young man's hand and thank him for dropping by, the young man said, "But, sir, aren't you going to fire me?" The president's response was a lesson for all of us. "Absolutely not," he said. "I have just invested five million dollars in your education. Just don't make the same mistake again."

You've no doubt heard stories over the years of people who were called failures. Albert Einstein was called a failure when he flunked courses in math. Henry Ford was called a failure when he went broke at the age of forty. Considering that Walt Disney went broke seventy-eight times, how many times do you think he was called a failure?

One of the most inspiring stories I've ever heard involved Thomas Edison. When we think about him, we think about a man who was the consummate American success story. But what many don't know is that late in his career, he spent ten years developing what he called the "nickel alkaline storage battery." Through that period of time, his record and film production company was supporting the storage battery effort. Then one night the terrifying cry of "Fire!" echoed through the film plant. Spontaneous combustion had ignited some chemicals. Within moments all of the packing compounds, the celluloid for his records and film, and other flammable goods had gone up in flames. Fire companies from eight towns arrived, but the heat was so intense and the water pressure so low that the fire hoses had no effect. Edison was sixty-seven years old, which was no age to begin anew.

His daughter was frantic, wondering if he was safe, if his spirit was broken, if he could handle a crisis that, in an instant, had made the great man penniless. But when she saw him, he started running toward her. He said, "Where's your mother? Go get her. Tell her to get her friends. They'll never see another fire like this as long as they live!" At five-thirty the next morning, with the fire barely under control, he called his employees together and announced, "We're rebuilding." One man was told to lease all the machine shops in the area, another to obtain a wrecking crane from the Erie Railroad Company.

Someone said to him, "But Mr. Edison, aren't you devastated that your life's work has just gone up in flames?"

"Oh, no," he said. "All my mistakes were destroyed in that fire, too. This is a rare opportunity to start all over."

As a matter of fact, virtually everything we now recognize as Edison's contribution to our lives came after that disaster. He very likely accomplished his best work because of his tragedy, not in spite of it. He learned to sense success even in midst of failure.

And he also realized something else that is so important for you to grasp for your own journey to the impossible: He realized he was in the wrong place at the right time. This sounds like another one of those difficult-to-grasp concepts, but it simply means that no matter what "wrong" situation you find yourself in—no matter what personal fire of your own you must deal with—you are being given a chance to learn a new set of skills, a new chance for success. I got this phrase from Shannon Sharpe, the All-Pro receiver for the Baltimore Ravens. During one of the Ravens' playoff games during their march to Super Bowl XXXV, a pass from quarterback Trent Dilfer bounced off the shoulders of the intended receiver, Jamal Lewis, bounced off the hands of a defending cornerback, and then bounced right into the hands of

Shannon Sharpe, who scampered down the sidelines fifty-eight yards for a touchdown. He later explained his good fortune by saying, "I was in the wrong place at the right time."

If you think about it, all great people have leveraged what other people said were their "failures." How do you explain the phenomenon of a Bill Gates, the richest man in America? For years, he found himself dismissed as a nerd with few skills whatsoever. He could have stopped his life and started calling himself a failure. Instead, he took advantage of his so-called weakness—being an unsocial computer nerd—and ended up having a far greater impact on the world's technology than any other genius you can name. At the opposite end of the spectrum, an elderly, frail, stooped-over nun named Mother Teresa, labeled a failure because she didn't fit in with the mainstream of life, ended up touching millions of people's lives in more than 100 nations through her small, quiet acts of giving. And how do you explain a little girl who was born to an unwed teenage mother, who was sexually abused at the age of nine by one uncle and at the age of eleven by another uncle? At the age of thirteen, she was put in a juvenile hall, and then kicked out because there wasn't enough room for her. Then, at fourteen, she followed in her mother's footsteps and had a baby of her own, one that was tragically stillborn. You might think this person I'm describing knew nothing in her life but failure and bitter disappointment—except that the person I've been describing is Oprah Winfrey, who turned out to be one of the most influential people in the United States.

When I broke my neck, I was in the wrong place, but I decided that it, too, would be my right time. I would not look at myself as a "failure," nor would I allow anyone else to look at me that way, either. I was going to leverage that failure. I was going to build on it.

So when you fail, relax. Fail again. Fail faster. You are doing wonders for yourself. There is no such thing as a failure; there is only an event that you may learn from. There are no mistakes in life, only lessons that will allow you to go farther and farther in your journey.

ELEVEN

❋

Stop Living on Your Little Island

STRATEGY: WHENEVER THERE IS CONFLICT IN YOUR LIFE, DON'T HIDE, BUT REACH OUT TO PEOPLE IMPORTANT TO YOU. THAT OLD CLICHÉ, "NO MAN IS AN ISLAND" CONTAINS MORE TRUTH THAN YOU MIGHT KNOW.

All too often I see a lot of people deal with significant changes in their lives by taking a step away from the world. They remove themselves from others as a form of self-protection. Or they are worried about being a burden on others.

Perhaps you've had this very idea when you've endured a tragedy or setback. You've lost your job or gone through a divorce and you've wanted to just, well, disappear. I know that in those initial days after my wreck, there were many times when I thought everything might be better if I was just left alone, because I was causing such pain and suffering for others.

But then people began to arrive—my fiancé, my family, my friends. On one level, I knew their hearts were broken, and I felt powerless to mend them. I looked at my father and said, "I'm sorry we wrecked your car. I'll get you a new one, I promise." I saw emotions rise to the surface in a man who was rarely emotional. Holding onto his shaky composure, he replied, "That's okay, son. You'll be all right," and he placed his big hand gently on my bruised shoulder. Then my mother, her pain written plainly across her beautiful face, leaned down and whispered those words about the difficult taking time and the impossible just taking a little longer.

And then came more friends and family, making the pilgrimage to my bedside in my hours of greatest need. They decorated my walls with signs declaring, "Get Well, Art." Colorful cards and messages were taped everywhere. The shelves above my bed were sagging under the weight of dozens of inspiring and motivational books. Flowers and green plants seemed to be growing from every corner. Balloons with streamers ascended from my headboard. Friends and family were with me around the clock, guardian angels whose love for me was deeper than I had previously known, and whose presence brought immeasurable strength and courage. They were there, too, when I left the hospital, always supportive, always comforting.

You might say, "Well, heck, Art, of course your friends didn't abandon you. What friends or family would?" I think you would be shocked to see the number of patients who suffered as I did in that hospital yet whose families never came and whose friends never visited. No flowers decorated their bedside tables. No cards colored the walls. These fellow sufferers had been dealt a tremendous blow in their lives, and no one cared enough to share that weight with them. I felt for them.

However, I also understood the great weight and burden my family carried by being there for me. If you questioned them about that today, they would all probably reply, "Oh, it was no big thing. We simply did what we needed to do." But I saw their pain every day. I saw the emotions held back as they sat with me. I saw their enthusiasm—and their heartbreak—as I learned how to wiggle my little finger again. I felt their emotions break again and again and again. But under the weight of difficult circumstances, our hearts were united in a unique and powerful way. And indeed, the results of this bonding became a significant and meaningful miracle in my struggling life.

None of us can be truly human in isolation. Life means nothing apart from other people. When you are faced with personal or professional tragedy, one of the first things you must do is reach out to others who can help—or who at least can be there for you.

I know that's not always an easy thing to do. Most of us spend our lives believing that independence and self-reliance are our most noble virtues. There are even some of us who have a streak of narcissism that believes we don't really need others. We're like Cain of the Old Testament, who scornfully snapped, "Am I my brother's keeper?" And what was Cain's punishment? He became a lonely wanderer on the face of the earth, with no place to call home, with no community to support or comfort him. He spent the rest of his days unconnected.

Is that you? When you fail, are you too humiliated or ashamed to ask for help? When you suffer, are you too embarrassed to ask for more support and comfort?

We have an ingrained prejudice, for some reason, against asking for help. We seem willing to dig ourselves into a deeper hole trying to fix a problem alone rather than asking for a little help. Others of us may realize that we need help but are unable to simply ask for it. Let me take it one step further. There are many of you who work so hard to be successful that it often corrodes your relationships with others. You begin to see others only in terms of what those people can do for you. There are some of you who even believe that winning in life means setting yourself against others. In your quest for power or money or fame, you tend to see life in terms of competition rather than cooperation.

But when facing life's challenges, one of the biggest mistakes you will make is to remove yourself from others. There is no one who knows enough to succeed independent of everyone else. Parents can learn from children; CEOs can learn from machine operators; managers can learn from new employees. While independence and self-reliance are noble virtues, interdependence and cooperation are far more valuable. Besides providing you with an emotional touchstone, friends, family, and others close to you are invaluable in helping you deal with the changes you face. Their concerns and ideas can be very important in your own problem-solving. It's like playing the game of Scrabble. You're staring at your seven letters, unable to see even a three-point, three-letter word. In defeat, you show the letters to your fellow players. To your surprise, they quickly come up with several high-scoring words you could have made. Several heads are better than one.

Maintaining good friends and close family relationships is as basic to life as air and water. Your friends and family can be like sheltering trees, protecting you from life's most battering storms. They weave a cocoon of love and friendship around you. Even when there is little they can do or say except to be there, their presence can be transcendent. Norman Hill, in his book *The Road Gets Rough,* told the story of a little boy who was sent on an errand by his mother and took longer than expected. When he returned, his mother questioned him about the delay.

The boy responded, "I met another boy whose tricycle was broken and who was crying because he couldn't fix it. So I helped him."

"But you don't know how to fix a tricycle," his mother said curiously.

"No, I don't," the young boy said, "so I sat down and cried with him."

For years, a favorite film of mine has been *It's a Wonderful Life*, starring Jimmy Stewart. It's the story of a man who spends his life helping others, but who suffers a devastating financial setback later in his years. At this point he contemplates that perhaps life would have been better for himself and others if he had never been born. In the end, his friends gather from everywhere to help him in his hour of need. The conclusion always makes my eyes fill with tears as a book is opened and on the front inside cover is written, "No man has failed who has friends."

I never appreciated that line more than on the day I left the hospital after four long months. A few days earlier, the bolts that had held my halo brace firmly in place against my head were removed. Alcohol was applied to the open wounds. At last, I was free. My collection of books, cards, dried flowers, and balloons was put into boxes. I slowly traveled the hallways and said my goodbyes to doctors, nurses, and other patients. Even though my stay in the hospital seemed like an eternity to me, I actually had been blessed with a speedy recovery. Many others with similar injuries would have to stay months longer. One gentleman I knew was hospitalized for more than a year before he was well enough to return home to his family and friends.

The inside of our small car was loaded to the ceiling with my belongings as we pulled away from the hospital into the busy street. I was on the outside now. Only memories and physical scars remained to remind me of my hospital days. Now I looked longingly out of the car window as we passed from my childhood city of San Jose toward the green hills of Hollister, where my family now resided. I found my mind drifting into an unknown future. How would I be accepted? What would I do? Every scene that passed by my window looked so different now. Where once I saw streets, stoplights, and people, now I focused on curbs, obstacles, ramps, and friendly faces within a crowd who might be willing to lend a helping hand when I needed it. Outside the care and protection of the hospital, my life was my own again. Life wasn't being lived in a bottle anymore. This was the real world, with no more conceptualizing and no more theoretical conversations. This was a new reality, and my future hinged on it. What I would become was up to me. I had a lot to think about.

The welcoming Hollister countryside was fragrant and green, and the slight breeze cooled the air perfectly. I felt exhilarated. As we came closer to home, I saw a huge banner across the front of the house, complete with balloons and streamers. The trees and bushes all over the yard cast a yellow glow, since they had all been filled with little yellow ribbons. Tears welled up in my eyes as friends and family members came to the curb to give me their special welcome. It seemed that the whole neighborhood had come. They had prayed for me, thought of me, and cried for me, and now they wanted to welcome me home.

A big potluck lunch was served in the back yard. We ate and laughed and talked, and as were finishing, some of the family and guests gathered to play a game of croquet. This was my chance, I thought, for me to begin my journey back into this new world. But when I tried to hold a mallet in my hands, my grasp was too weak to hit anything besides myself. With a little creativity, we figured out the most advantageous means for me to be able to play. I watched, with some courage and a good sense of humor, as my family secured the mallet to my forearm with sticky tape. Now I was armed and dangerous! They wheeled me around the yard, and with just the right angle, I'd swing the mallet with as much force as I could. Sometimes I made my mark, but mostly I hit the grass, my wheelchair, or someone else.

Then came time to take a tour of our home, which never looked so good. A long sloping ramp extended from the door of the house. My brother had given up his ground-floor bedroom for my convenience. I was so touched by the generosity of my family. Still, I felt like a child who sees everything as new. My world looked so different than it had before. Immediately, I noticed the simple things, such as the height of doorknobs, cabinet shelves, clothes rods in the closets, light switches, desks, and tables. I noticed the width of hallways, door frames, and shower stalls, and also the problem of stairs.

We had a plush carpet throughout much of our home. It was soft to the feet, but in my manual wheelchair it felt as if I was pushing through sand. Every push required a great deal of energy and effort. I could only push an inch or two before requiring some rest. It took me half an hour or more to get from one end of the hallway to the other. Those familiar words echoed in my ears: "You must use an electric wheelchair, Art. To get around this hospital on smooth linoleum floors is one thing, but for you to challenge the world without the use of a motor is not very feasible." But I wouldn't complain. I knew that in time my strength would return. Effort always precipitates growth.

The learning process had just begun. One of my first big goals had been to get down the ramp to the back yard without requiring help. Because of the restrictions of space, it was a short, rather steep ramp that led directly into a flowerbed and tree. Each day I had my little brother, Roger, pull back on the wheelchair as I went down the ramp. As he would resist gravity, I would strain to help keep the chair at a controllable speed. Each day Roger complimented me on my improvement. Finally, one day I thought I could do it by myself. Being a cautious person, I did ask Roger to walk behind me and help only if I was getting out of control. He agreed, but the fact was that he knew there was no way I could do it on my own. Quietly, saying nothing, he helped me all the way down. At the bottom of the ramp, wanting me to feel a sense of accomplishment, he told me proudly that he hadn't helped at all. I had done it on my own, he said.

I swelled with such a false sense of achievement that the next morning I eagerly asked my mother to come see the great thing I had learned. I knew she'd be proud. Asking her to stand at the bottom of the steep ramp, I told her I was going to demonstrate how I could get down by myself.

"Are you sure you can do this, Art?" she asked.

"Absolutely," I confidently replied. "Besides, I had Roger standing behind me yesterday in case I needed help, and I didn't need him at all. Just stand there and watch me go." I slowly pushed off. Instantly, gravity took over and I began gaining momentum. I was shocked at the amount of speed I picked up so quickly. I held harder against the hand rims. I still went faster. Almost as quickly as I had begun, I was at the bottom, racing toward my mother, who now had a look of terror in her eyes.

"Stop me, Mom!" I yelled. She reached forward to try and slow me down. Too late. I hit her just below the knees at full speed, sending both of us flying into the flowers and trees.

"I thought you said you had it all under control!" Mother exclaimed.

"I did. Yesterday, Roger said . . ." I paused and thought for a moment, then both of us went to find Roger. We all had a good laugh, even though it was mostly at my expense.

The point of these anecdotes is to help you understand that when life becomes a struggle, there is no better life preserver than the love of people close to you. And one of the most valuable lessons I learned was that help will always come from the most unexpected sources. Whenever Dallas and I went out on the town together, we were sometimes overwhelmed by people's willingness to help. One night, we went to a movie theater that had a number of steep steps that must be climbed if you wanted good seats. I sat at the bottom of those steps for a moment, before two kind gentlemen— total strangers—offered their assistance. Following the movie, instead of quickly leaving, they searched me out to help me down the stairs again.

The men were big, tough, tattoo-laden bikers with the smell of cigarettes and alcohol on their breath. They were the kind of men often ignored or rejected by society. In the past I would have rejected them, too. But they had big hearts. The depth of their compassion deeply touched me.

If I had been full of too much pride—if I had remained an island—I would have remained completely incapable of doing much at all in my new life as a quadriplegic. I would have crippled my capabilities and limited my potential. But it's the beautiful tapestry of relationships that provides life richer meaning. For me, I was never so blessed with richer and more beautiful meaning than June 18th, 1985, a year and a half after my accident. The sun was shining that day brighter and more beautifully than on any other day I can remember. The sky was a deep, azure blue and the wind blew lightly, bringing with it the fragrance of nearby flowers. Friends and family had gathered on the green lawns of the Salt Lake Latter Day Saints Temple. The day had come for Dallas and myself. We were about to be married.

For five years, we had laughed and experienced life together, and we had never once dreamed of being apart. To be together meant everything to us. It was our world. Together, our greatest ambitions, dreams, and most righteous desires bubbled to the surface. Every moment together was a new thrill in discovery and understanding. It seemed that the more we were together, the more we wanted to stay that way forever.

I had brought Dallas with me to California in August 1983 under the guise of showing her the new business I was getting involved in. With an engagement ring burning a hole in my pocket, I was ready to officially ask Dallas to be my wife. Parking near the oceanfront of Carmel, a quaint, romantic town, I suggested, "Let's go down to the beach. It's a nice evening, we can go for a walk." This was the event I had dreamed of for years. I wanted the proposal to be special—and what could be more romantic than a walk along a white-sand beach with the waves gently rolling in and the moonlight casting its reflection across the miles of water?

There was just one problem: As we trudged toward the beach through the thick sand, I noticed right away that it was rather dark. The moon wasn't out. However, I wouldn't let my plans be frustrated. I said, "Dallas, let's walk over there." Standing next to a tree near the front entrance to the men's room, I was ready. The light was just right for me to present my proposal. (A little awkward, but at least there was light!) Standing Dallas squarely in front of me, and looking her in the eye, I asked, "Dallas, will you be my forever princess?" A half-smile came across her face, but she was still not registering exactly what I meant. Desiring to make my intentions clear I responded, "This is a proposal, just in case you're wondering."

A beautiful smile replaced her look of confusion. She beamed brightly and blushed. Our dreams—or so we thought—were about to come true.

But then came the accident, and we found ourselves thrown together into a nightmare that neither of us had anticipated. The weeks before a wedding date should have been moments one remembers with a broad smile for years to come, not with a face twisted with pain and pillows soaked with tears. The day before Dallas was to leave for California to be with me at the hospital, she ran into an old friend. Dallas told the friend that the wedding plans had been delayed because of my serious automobile accident.

"Does that mean he is in a wheelchair?" the friend asked.

"Yes, that was the prognosis, but I know he won't be in it forever."

With a puzzled look on her face, the friend asked, "Well, I'm sure you're not going to still marry him—are you? I mean, how could you, with the way things are now?"

Her question took Dallas completely off guard. For a moment, Dallas wasn't sure whether to take her seriously. But then Dallas looked her friend straight in the eyes and said that she couldn't imagine life not being married to me, and she felt very blessed to still have me.

Dallas was at my side almost every day in the hospital. She made every sacrifice to be there with me. She moved permanently from her family and friends in Utah to California, a place often unfriendly and threatening to newcomers. She took a job in a place where she could be near the hospital, and she lived in my friend's home close by. Void of her usual crowd of friends and associates, she made my bedside her home, and her nightlife was in the dim, arid, smelly halls of the hospital.

Someone has said that "The same winds snuff out candles, yet kindle fires; so where adversity kills a little love, it fans a great one." The cold winds of pain and struggle were blowing relentlessly in our lives. An instantaneous miracle in the beginning—the miracle of being allowed to walk again—could have sheltered us from the harsh influence of that storm, but what would we have given up? As the winds blew day after day, Dallas and I enjoyed benefits we never before could have imagined—more enriched communication, a widened perspective of who we were, a deeper understanding of our needs, an enhanced tolerance, a strengthened commitment, and more solidified dreams. During one short struggling period of time, we learned what a thousand hours of marriage seminars could not teach.

Of course, we were disappointed at the unexpected delay of our wedding plans, but we also knew that our love could not be denied forever. But on that June 1985 afternoon, our months and years of dreaming were about to become a reality. The love I felt in my heart was unsurpassed by anything I had ever felt before in my life. Dressed in white, I sat in the quiet beauty of the hallway waiting to enter the marriage room. As I wheeled myself in, I was overwhelmed by so many hopes and dreams being fulfilled. As I saw Dallas, clothed in the wedding dress that had waited so long for its bride, I fell in love with her all over again.

The gentleman who was to perform the ceremony offered to let me remain in my wheelchair for the ceremony. However, I felt I had to kneel; it was a dream I had promised myself to fulfill on that day. My two brothers, holding me under my arms, gently lifted me from my chair, and helped me kneel at that altar. Holding Dallas's warm hand, I looked into her glowing eyes and smiled.

The words I only faintly recall today. But the feeling I will never forget. We both wept as the words of the ceremony were spoken. For us, a true miracle had taken place. We were together.

TWELVE

❋

Ask Better Questions

STRATEGY: LEARN TO TALK TO YOURSELF
IN A WAY THAT GIVES YOU BETTER
ANSWERS FOR YOUR LIFE

In his book *Awaken the Giant Within,* Tony Robbins stated that the "quality of our lives is equal to the quality of the questions we ask ourselves." Every day we are constantly asking ourselves questions. "What time do I have to get up this morning?" "What happens if I don't get up?" "What am I going to wear today?" (Some people, of course, spend more time on that one than any other.) The point is, we are always asking questions of ourselves. That is just the way our minds work—through questions.

The kinds of questions we ask often have a lot to do with the quality of the answers we are getting. I have learned several things from this idea:

1. You cannot get an answer to a question you've never asked. Sometimes we are afraid to ask certain questions, because either we fear the answer or we don't have the disposition to find the truth on our own. The failure to ask certain questions can lead to disastrous conclusions. People who smoke often avoid the question of what the long-term effects may be for their lives and loved ones. That can have a disastrous result. If you are afraid to ask the question, there is a pretty good chance you are heading for trouble.

2. If you want a better answer, then ask a better question. There are many people who are not afraid of asking questions. They are just frustrated by the quality of the answers they have been getting. When this is the case, it is often because we are not looking for solutions as much as we are looking for someone to blame. Sometimes we just want to be angry and need only enough information to justify it. When we do this, we are asking questions with the intent to get "specific answers," not necessarily the truth.

3. The worst way to ask a question much of the time is to begin it with the word "why." A better way to ask a question is to begin all of them with either "what" or "how." Here are some examples: "What can I learn from this experience?" "How can I put myself into a position to rise about this experience?" "What can I do differently the next time?" "How can I take advantage of these circumstances to make an opportunity for myself?"

I often call people who ask these questions "harvesters." As opposed to the "why-ners" (those who focus on the pain they have endured by asking why they have endured it), harvesters envision what they can do with their pain and predicaments to improve the quality of their lives. Harvesters focus on the outcome of their crop, not on the storms that sometimes loom overhead. They ask quality questions in order to get quality answers.

My father was always trying to get me to ask harvester questions. He had little tolerance for any of my excuses when I was growing up. If I came home and said, "Dad, my teachers never believe me. They're saying I didn't turn in my homework, but I did," he'd reply, "What they're saying is your problem. What have you done in the past that would lead them to distrust you? What can you do in the future to establish mutual respect? This isn't their problem, it's yours. Now what are you going to do about it?"

One day, soon after I had received my driver's license as a teenager, I was rear-ended by another driver who was plainly at fault. "Dad, someone rear-ended the car," I said when I got home. He only replied, "What could you have done to have kept him from rear-ending you?" Back then, I could not get at all what he was talking about. "What could I have done?" I declared. "Dad, it wasn't my fault!" "It might not have been your fault, but it's your responsibility," he replied. "So you need to ask yourself what you have to do to keep people from doing the same thing to you again. Maybe you need to look more in the rearview mirror and make sure you are staying well in front of other cars."

My father used the harvester technique in his own life. After completing high school, he went into the Navy for four years, where he received training in electronics. After an honorable dis charge from the Navy he went to work for IBM in Poughkeepsie, New York. He worked for IBM for twenty-three years, receiving many promotions based on the results he produced. But my father's boss came to him one day and said, "Dave, I am not sure how you got this far at IBM with your limited education, but if you want to be promoted again you should go back to school."

My father never asked why he was being treated in such a way. He didn't spend time figuring out who to blame. He asked himself, "What can I do about this problem?" He decided to quit. He quickly got a job at Memorex as a director of information systems, and later he was recruited by Sun Microsystems as a vice president. Today he is a chief information officer for a $500 million company and is regarded as one of the best in the world at what he does. And incidentally, he didn't go back to school.

I had to develop my ability to ask harvester questions when I returned to the workplace after my stay in the hospital. Do you remember how the doctors told me I would never work again? "Don't even think about work again, Art," said a doctor, "because ninety-three percent of those in your condition never do." I was determined to prove him wrong, and in fact, six months after my accident, I reopened the doors of my tennis court construction company. In one regard, I was extremely fortunate. Dallas's brother, Scott, was willing to come to California to work as my associate. He supervised construction of the courts while I ran the business, planned and executed marketing strategies, and kept the books. After two successful years, we sold the company and I went to find a new place in the workforce.

Before life in the wheelchair, finding employment was easy. But I knew my first job hunt since my accident would require great effort, a lot of planning, and time. I spent many hours scouring newspapers, calling employers, setting up interviews, and meeting with representatives of different companies. The story seemed like a never-ending circle. On the phone they would sound enthusiastic and promising regarding my qualifications, anxious for me to be a part of their team and sometimes almost even hiring me before we had a chance to interview. But then into their office I would roll, and their enthusiasm would turn to disappointment and, perhaps, fright.

At one point, after the search for a sales job kept hitting dead ends, I met with an experienced employment agency that assists physically limited people in getting jobs. Although they were very competent at what they do, they discouraged me from any further search in the sales field. They insisted that I was expecting too much. Who would hire a quadriplegic to sell their products when they had plenty of able-bodied applicants to choose from? They asked me to lower my sights.

And so, because I needed to work—and because I wanted to work—I applied for the position of a telephone operator for an IBM message center.

After several interviews with key people, and my list of usual promises and commitments, IBM said they would accept me if I had adequate typing competency. The job required a typing speed of no less than forty words per minute. On the morning of the test, I was piled into a room with several others who would be testing as well. With my hand-made typing splints firmly on my two index fingers, I began typing. Five minutes later, the buzzer sounded the end of our test. I had passed—just barely. I was offered a three-month temporary position with IBM. With superior performance, that period could be extended to six months.

My new job consisted of taking internal messages for any of 9,000 employees at that plant site. I worked at a terminal along with about fifteen other people. Our performance was measured by how many messages we were able to take each day. The phones would ring continually. As soon as you were done receiving a message for one person, the phone was ringing with the next. I took over 300 messages every day that I worked there, sometimes even exceeding 400, which broke previous records. Finally, I was given my three-month extension.

I was grateful for the temporary work, but after a few weeks, I began asking myself more questions. I asked if this really was promising work with a future. I needed a healthy income to meet my financial obligations. I needed good benefits, including medical coverage. I needed a suitable work environment to meet the requirements of life in a wheelchair. And I needed a workplace that wasn't too far from home. My needs were great, and my job counselors said I was dreaming if I thought I could find such a job.

Nevertheless, I started searching. I looked again among computer sales companies. I was met with rejection wherever I turned. Some simply never called back. Others told me very directly that because I was in a wheelchair, I would not even be considered, regardless of any past achievements or sales records. They openly wondered how I would do such minor tasks as get myself to the offices of other customers.

The truth was that for the first year after leaving the hospital, transportation had been a serious problem. I did need to be chauffeured from place to place. Dallas would help me into the passenger seat, fold up my chair, and load it into the back of the car. When I was in the car, there was no "running in" anyplace. Everywhere we went required enormous effort and time. And bad weather made getting places even more difficult.

But less than two years after my accident, this whole picture changed. My strength and abilities had improved to the point that we had a van built especially for my needs. When it first pulled into my driveway, I could hardly contain my enthusiasm. It had a hydraulic lift on the side door to get me and my wheelchair inside, a raised roof for my height, a driver's seat that pivoted completely around so that I could climb into it, and hand controls that operated the brake and accelerator. Riding the lift up for the first time, I felt like an eight-year-old boy on Christmas morning.

The real test came, however, when I had to transfer myself into the driver's seat. While I had developed enough strength during the last year to push myself successfully from place to place, lifting my 150-pound body was a different matter. Resisting offers of help, I struggled, groaned, and pushed as I tried to lift my body out of the wheelchair and into that seat. Twenty minutes later I was in the new seat and preparing to drive for the first time since my accident. Learning to drive again with just my hands was a unique experience. It felt like playing a video game—only the other drivers on the road didn't exactly think it was a game. After practicing in very large, empty parking lots, I began to brave the real world. It was a thrill beyond words. Not only had new worlds of opportunity opened up for me, but once again, I had defied a group of naysayers: the doctors who told me I would never drive again.

Still, my hunt for a job was going nowhere. If there was a time to start asking why, to start blaming, to start living in the past or the future, this was it. I could have shouted out, "Hey, look at all the hard work I've done since my accident. Look how I'm able to do things with my body that no one told me I'd be able to do. Look how I'm able to feed myself. Look how I'm able to use a manual wheelchair. How about some appreciation here!"

But I had to continually take inventory and remind myself that blaming and "why-ning" were fruitless. To find excuses for everything only meant that I was getting further from the real answers. The worst lie we ever tell is to ourselves. I had to tell myself, "If you quit now, it's not someone else's fault. It's your fault." I had to continually say, "I am one hundred percent responsible for my life."

And I had to make sure I was asking myself the right questions that would lead me to what I wanted.

During the lowest period of my own job search, I renewed my drive to ask harvester-like questions. "What can I do today which will have the most impact on my career?" "What do I need to do to change my communication skills more effectively?" "What can I do or say right now to calm the fears of those who are interviewing me?"

I began exerting even a greater effort to sell myself. I attacked potential employers' concerns up front, inviting their questions and objections, making them open up about all their anxieties they were having just at the sight of me. To alleviate their concerns about my capabilities, I would offer to work for free for two weeks, even a month. I told them if I could not perform as well as if not better than, their number-one producer within one month, I would gladly leave their employ of my own accord.

Many employers were impressed with my willingness to sacrifice, but their levels of trust and belief were aptly displayed through their lack of return phone calls or follow-up interviews. Once again, I could have said, "Well, so much for the harvesting technique. I'm going home." But then I asked myself another series of "what" questions. "What will be the pain if I don't keep going? What will be the ultimate price if I don't follow through? What will it cost me emotionally, physically, financially, spiritually?"

And so I kept looking. I kept telling myself that I didn't have to choose the same feelings that others have when they hit roadblocks—feelings of fear and discouragement and hopelessness. I kept telling myself that it was my choice either to let these roadblocks be dead ends, or to turn them into minor obstacles that I eventually could get around. I also kept telling myself, "With each rejection and denial will come benefits of greater value." The struggle itself to find a job was making me a better person. I had become more determined, more willing to bang on shut doors, more adamant about people seeing who I really was.

Following dozens of interviews with technical companies, the phone call finally came from Bell Atlantic CompuShop. "Art, we'd be excited to have you on our team. Can you start on Monday?" Tears flowed down my cheeks. To the world, another small sales job had been filled. To me, another miracle had transpired. Once again, I had a future I could build on.

THIRTEEN

Why Are You Obsessing About Your Goals?

Strategy: Goal-Setting Is Great,
But What's More Important
Is Setting a Vision of Who You Want to Be

When I was formulating a plan on how to rebuild my life, I read a series of books on goal-setting. The problem was that just about every book was different. One book told me to set ten big goals in my life. Another book said I should only have five goals. Then another book told me no, I should have three goals for each of the following areas of my life—financial, relationship, spiritual, personal, physical, and emotional. Then I found a book that told me to have some "short-term goals" and some "long-term goals."

There was one common theme to all of those books, however.

They said I should remain very focused on my goals, stick diligently to them, and develop that never-give-up, never-say-die, never-ever-quit mentality about achieving them. I came away from those books thinking that once you set a goal, you see it through—and that's what I was going to do. My tennis court business is a perfect example. Even though I realized after my accident that my ambition to build tennis courts was not exactly what I wanted to do for the rest of my life, even though my heart wasn't fully in it, I felt obligated to pursue it because it had been my "goal."

Don't misunderstand. I am very proud of what I was able to do. Resurrecting that company and making it viable provided me great satisfaction, as did getting my job in computer sales. Every month that I was with the company I either met or exceeded my pre-set sales quota. I received national sales awards on three different occasions for my sales skills and achievements. When the company found it necessary to reduce its sales force by nearly 60 percent, I was one of two salesmen retained in our region. The seemingly impossible had, once again, become reality.

But even then, I knew I wasn't ultimately where I wanted to be. I had reached a goal—proving that I could be just as competent a salesman as anyone else—but it wasn't a business where I felt rooted. Nor was it the kind of business that would ever let me become financially independent. True, attaining the "goal" of excellence in sales had given me an unshakeable new confidence. But I realized that the "goal," while admirable, had not been what I completely wanted for my life.

So, leaving the experience of three and a half years of computer sales behind me, Dallas and I moved to Utah, where I set another goal: I wanted to own my own business. I opened a bookstore that sold mostly inspirational and motivational books and tapes. Soon I opened two more bookstores and was asked to manage eleven more. I enjoyed it immensely, I did well, but again, it occurred to me that this goal wasn't enough.

During the entire time I was doing these other jobs, I had been speaking, mostly to teenagers at youth conferences and at summer camps. I don't know if I was popular, but I was free, which turned out to be a very valuable marketing tip. Not long after my release from the hospital, I told Dallas that I wanted to teach an early-morning religious studies class at our local church. Dallas had stared at me with the thought clearly written in her eyes, "But Art, how are you going to do it?" At the time, I had no idea. That was during a period when I couldn't even begin to dress myself. But I said I had to try. The class began at 6:15 every weekday morning. To get to the church and get the classroom set up, I needed to leave my home before 5:30 A.M. The first morning of class, I arose at 2:30 A.M. to begin getting dressed. For the next two and a half hours, I used every available resource—teeth, arms, shoulders, and hands with fingers that refused to work—struggling to put on my clothes. But by 5:30 that morning, physically exhausted and emotionally spent, I sat dressed and ready to teach.

As the years passed, I was able to get my dressing time down to twenty minutes. But the point of the story is that I was willing to go to great lengths in those early years for the opportunity to talk, tell stories, and articulate ideas. I felt a similar exhilaration when I spoke to youth groups. With each speech, my stories became more relevant, and my audiences became more responsive. The number of speeches continued to grow. The audiences got larger and larger. Soon I was speaking in high school gymnasiums to thousands of students. In time, my content became more diverse. Not only was I talking about attitude, but now I was talking about life skills, peer pressure, and making decisions that last. The word continued to spread, and soon I was being asked to travel to give speeches. On one occasion, I drove for three hours into the mountains of Utah to speak at a girls' camp with fifty participants. As usual, the experience was gratifying. But on the long drive back home I wondered how much longer I could keep this up. Fulfilling my new "goal"—which was running a retail business—was taking its toll on my time and energy. Dallas and I were also planning to start our family. Something had to give. With some reluctance and emotional angst, I decided to turn down all future speaking requests.

Coincidentally, or perhaps divinely, a friend of mine suggested that I sell my bookstores and speak for a living. I looked at him. Such an idea had never occurred to me before. It was a significant risk to even think about changing professions. My retail business was growing. The income was steady and stabilizing. I had just been recognized by the Small Business Administration as one of its young entrepreneurs of the year. And now I was going to give it all up?

Nevertheless, I thought about the idea. I found myself having financial analysts evaluate the worth of my retail business if I sold it, and I discovered that I wouldn't be able to get nearly as much for it as I had thought. But then I attended an annual convention of the National Speakers Association in Palm Desert, California. More than 900 professional speakers were in attendance. I sat in the back of a large ballroom and listened intently. Before long I thought, "I can do this."

Then came another interesting turn of events. A manager from a local company, Novell, called and asked if I would be willing to speak at an awards banquet. I agreed. He asked how much I would charge. That was a new question for me. I answered questioningly, "How about fifty bucks?" He started laughing.

"Uh-oh," I thought. "That's too high!"

Then the manager said, "I am going to tell my boss you charge five hundred dollars so that I don't embarrass you or me."

I hung up thinking, "Wow, five hundred dollars for an hour!" I was ready to turn pro right then.

But more important was the idea that I was going to try something that always had made me feel at my best. I was going to get the opportunity to make a lasting difference in the lives of other people. It sounds odd, but the very thing that I realized I was meant to do—to speak—I had been doing all along, and I hadn't even seen it.

Goal-setting is important. It is a wonderful way to focus your attention and drive you forward. What happened to me, however, was that I became driven more by my goal-setting than by my vision of who I should be as a person and what I should be doing that brought out the best of me.

Your vision for yourself is what you know you need to make your life significant. Goals don't do that. Goals can make you feel as if you have "achieved" something. But they cannot make you happier. Goals are your way of knowing that you've reached certain landmarks over a certain period of time. But they cannot make you feel more worthy. You can say, for instance, "I made my goal of selling a million dollars in product this year." But you can't say, "That million dollars has made me the person I want to be."

In fact, let's say you set a financial goal of making $1 million by the time you are forty years old. It's the kind of goal you see lots of other authors suggest that you have—a standard, solid goal that no one can argue with, right? The problem is, that goal might not be congruent with your vision for your life. If your vision is to have the freedom to enjoy life, the work that's going to be required to make that million dollars could rob you of that very vision. You won't have time to relax, to be with your family or at your church or involved in your community. Once you get the million dollars, you might be able to relax, but what cost would you have paid to get there?

Late in his life, Walt Disney, who solved more business and artistic problems than most of us are ever likely to confront, was asked to share his secret of success. Disney didn't talk about setting goals. He talked about the importance of discovering a vision for yourself. He said the first thing one should do to be successful is to think about his or her beliefs and values. Disney said the quality of a person's life derives, in large measure, from those very things. He added that the clearer one's understanding of his or her own values, beliefs, convictions, and philosophies are, the easier it becomes to make the difficult choices and decisions about how to live one's life. If one believes deeply in an idea, a cause, and a purpose, then one can believe in oneself.

The most successful people are not the ones with the most number of goals, nor are they the ones who can tell you how many of their goals they have met. They are people who work hard at living up to a vision of themselves. Their goals are part of what they do to live up to that vision. In other words, you must have a personal calling, a sense of mission, a quest. Then, if you act in a manner consistent with those beliefs, no matter what, you can begin to receive what you truly want most out of life. If you don't have that vision down, and you are not operating off that vision, then you could find yourself trying to accomplish one goal after another—making money, buying a nice home, moving to another city, getting a more prestigious job, traveling, whatever—without finding any real satisfaction except to say, "Look what I accomplished."

Sometimes you have to do what I did, which is to explore things to find your way. But always remember, when you set a goal at the very outset, you might not have the wisdom and insight to say, "This is not the right goal. There's another place I should be going in my life." You need to be flexible about your goals. At first I wasn't flexible at all. Because my company's name is Invictus—"unconquered, unsubdued, invincible"—I thought I would not be living up to that name if I gave up on my goals. But now I know that goals serve a specific purpose—to measure your progress and help keep you on track toward your vision. If that goal is not sharpening that vision—if it is becoming overwhelming, or distracting, or making you feel you are doing drudgery-like work just to accomplish it—then perhaps the time has come to change that goal.

Think about it this way: Goals tend to help you get to a place that already is, rather than help you create a better vision of yourself that does not yet exist. So before you set goals, make sure you know the answer to these three simple questions:

1. *What do you genuinely love?*
2. *What are you completely passionate about?*
3. *What do you really want?*

I know that for some of you it's hard to articulate what your vision for yourself might be. You find it difficult to say what it is you truly want to do or how you want to be. So what you might try first is recognize the emotions that drive your desires. In other words, what particular quality of life do you want? If one of your desires, for instance, is to become a millionaire, then ask yourself what you believe is the underlying emotional need for that million dollars. Is it security? Peace of mind? Public recognition? Maybe your deepest desires are serenity, connection with God, a desire to lead others, a desire for freedom.

You can make many lists. You might want to write down specific things you want to do before you die. Perhaps it's to travel to

France and drink fine wine; perhaps it's to work for a summer as a missionary. You might write down a list of five occupations you'd like to try. You might write down what you'd do with yourself if you had a single year when you could do anything you wanted and no one would be watching. You might write a list of your favorite day-dreams, or write a list of the things that always makes you smile. As you read over your lists, you'll realize you are looking at the clues to the vision of yourself.

One other technique you might try is to write a version of what companies call their "mission statement." Almost every company I know has a set of guiding principles that clearly state its philosophy and its goals. It's a wonderful tool for companies. Whenever they get into major policy meetings and they wonder if a particular proposal is what they want, they sometimes pull out their mission statements and read them. As a board member and officer for the National Speakers Association, before we conduct any strategy sessions or official business, we review our stated vision, mission, and values. They can be very simple, but they remind the company precisely what matters most to them. And that's exactly what your own personal mission statement could do. It is there to make sure you are headed in the right direction. It is like automobile headlights, illuminating your destination. It is there to remind you that if you try to be the best you can be as a human being, then everything else will follow.

Make sure your personal mission statement embodies your deepest values, not just your goals. Perhaps you want to be a great, powerful leader; perhaps you want to be a doctor; perhaps you want to get involved in a real career for the first time in your life in order to prove to yourself and others that you can make money on your own; perhaps you want to get your Ph.D.; perhaps you want to run a charity ball; perhaps you want to get into super athletic shape; perhaps you want to learn how to speed-read 3,000 words per minute so you can read more novels; perhaps you want to save $30,000 in the next few years to start a college education fund for your children; perhaps you want to learn Spanish.

Whatever your desire is: Great! No dream you cherish is too grand or too insignificant. No arena you strive to excel in is too large or too small.

But your personal mission statement is designed to emphasize the underlying reason why you want to change. If you want to become a doctor, then maybe it is because your deepest desire is to help others. If you want to become a leader, then maybe it is because your deepest desire is to develop your character to the fullest.

Try to articulate your own vision in a personal mission statement. Even if it's vague, it is the very thing that can keep you on course for the rest of your life. When you are at a crossroads, you can think of your vision and ask if you are giving your best effort to bringing all those qualities into your life.

FOURTEEN

✳

Don't Let One Bad Day Turn into a Bad Life

STRATEGY: WHEN DAYS GET TOUGH, TAKE A BREAK.
RELY ON THE "POWER OF THE PAUSE."
GIVE UP FIGHTS THAT YOU CAN'T WIN.

D o you know how the little hassles that crop up during a day can often undermine your emotional disposition? Here you are, filled with big dreams, big ideas for new projects, big plans and goals, and you find yourself sitting on the side of the highway during the afternoon, waiting for the tow truck to arrive to fix your broken-down car.

One of the great victories in life is to be able to stay focused on the big issues by not letting daily trivial irritations overwhelm you. As a professional speaker, I travel quite a bit for a living—200,000 miles or more a year. And when I travel, I encounter a variety of transportation challenges. True, the Americans with Disabilities

Act, passed in 1992, did make access easier for me and the more than 48 million Americans who are disabled. Because of the act, transportation was simplified, hotel rooms were made more accessible, more elevators were installed, and street curbs were lowered. Also as part of that legislation, major car rental companies began renting cars with hand controls for people such as myself. So on a trip to Boston, I decided to try it out. I rented a car, went out into the dark parking lot at the Logan Airport in Boston, located my car, opened the trunk, and put my bags inside. I was proud of myself. It was the first time I had ever done that alone. I opened the car door, transferred myself into the driver's seat, disassembled my wheelchair, pulled it over my body, and placed it in the seat next to me. Wow! Another first.

But then I encountered my first major problem. While the car was an automatic, the gearshift was located between the seats. In order to get the transmission to release from Park, you had to press the button on the bottom of the gearshift and pull back. Keep in mind, I had one hand on the hand control for the brake, and one hand on the gearshift. Also bear in mind that as a quadriplegic, I have no finger function in my hands. It was impossible with one hand to pull up on the button and pull back into Drive.

I thought about it for a moment and came up with an idea. What if I used two hands: one to pull up on the button, the other to pull back on the gear shift? I wondered if I could get the car into Drive and get my left hand back to the brake before my car hit the one in front of me. I figured, "Hey, I got the insurance option!"

My plan worked, which then led to my second major problem. Without full use of my hands, it was difficult turning the steering wheel. I have to put pressure against the steering wheel with the palm of my hand to turn. Brand-new cars, as this one was, have very slick steering wheels. I could turn to the left okay, I was just having trouble turning to the right. I thought about it for a moment and then realized, "If you take enough lefts, it is just like taking a right!" It took me a while to get out of the parking lot, but I did it. An irritating hassle became a victory.

Although it's important not to let the little irritations consume you, it's also important not to ignore them. Backing down when others are unfairly running over you, or giving up with a sigh, can ultimately cause more distress than the hassle did in the first place. So I make sure to deal with them. I was sitting on an airplane some time ago preparing to fly to a speaking engagement. I had been assigned a window seat, which was my preference. Sitting at the window, a flight attendant approached me and said, "I'm sorry, sir, but you can't sit by the window."

"Really? And why is that?" I asked with a smile.

"It's in case of an emergency," she said with authority.

"I'm sorry," I responded, "I didn't know you needed help."

Unimpressed with my attempts to be funny, she stated, "I'm sorry sir, but it is an FAA regulation that you sit in the aisle seat. In the event of an emergency it will be easier for us to get to you."

"I'm not sure where you heard that it was an FAA regulation," I answered, "but it is not. Before I move, I would like to see the regulation you are referring to in writing."

She walked back to the front of the plane and began quickly turning the pages of her FAA handbook. A few minutes later she returned. "I have not been able to find the specific regulation yet. However, if you move to the aisle now so that we can go ahead and take off I will look for it in flight."

Here was the issue. Should I be passive and move, or should I stand up for myself, perhaps helping someone else to avoid a similar challenge in the long run? I reasoned, "I will be happy to move after you can show me the regulation in writing." She returned to the front, obviously unhappy, scanned through her handbook, and then returned a few moments later she returned. "I'm sorry. You are correct. It is not an FAA regulation."

I gave her a smile and said, "Absolutely no problem." And then I enjoyed my view from the window as the plane lifted into the sky.

Ironically, only two weeks later, I was on a different flight heading toward a different city. This time I was sitting in an aisle seat. Suddenly, a flight attendant approached and said, "I am sorry, sir, but you cannot sit in the aisle seat."

Again, I tried humor. "A couple of weeks ago I was told I couldn't sit in the the window seat. I am just curious, why can't I sit in the aisle seat?"

"Sir, in the event of an emergency, the passenger seated next to you will not be able to get to the aisle to escape."

I replied, "The gentleman sitting next to me looks somewhat athletic. I am fairly certain that in the event of an emergency he could leap over me." The passenger seated next to me nodded enthusiastically in the affirmative. Continuing with my absurd point, I made the observation, "As I have been sitting here watching passengers board the plane I am fairly certain that some of them are stupid. In the event of an emergency I would be willing to bet that stupid people will go the wrong way, thus blocking the aisle for smart people. I think that we should administer an IQ test for all passengers as they board the plane so that we can be certain that the dumb ones are sitting by the windows." I would have continued, except that now a supervisor had come quickly to end the dialogue by telling the flight attendant that FAA regulations would let me sit wherever I wanted as long as it wasn't an exit row.

I finally figured I had all my airplane and rental car problems solved, until I arrived in Orlando recently to speak at a convention. It was the wearisome hour of 1:30 in the morning. I had reserved a car from one of the major car rental companies. (I might add that this company has had a history with me of providing outstanding service for many years prior to this unfortunate incident.) After retrieving my bags, I proceeded to the area where the shuttle bus would take me to the car rental lot. I was grateful that I was picked up by one of the newer buses that had a wheelchair lift on it to accommodate me. Once on the bus and situated where I needed to be, the driver proceeded to strap my wheelchair to the floor to ensure that it was secure while he drove. I did not have a problem with this. But then he began to put a three-point restraint system (a seat belt) across my lap and shoulders. I smiled and said that I would prefer not to wear the seat belt.

The driver was very hostile. He insisted that I wear it or I would have to find another way to the car rental lot. I asked him why, since there was no law requiring it. He replied that it was for my safety. I asked then why he wasn't concerned about the safety of the other six people on the bus, since they were not required to wear seat belts. One of the other passengers was a toddler. He stated that the toddler had her mother with her.

Okay, I know I've said to treat life's little irritations with humor, but I admit, this time, I thought a good dose of sarcasm might help. I said, "So, what you are telling me is that if I bring my mother with me the next time then I don't have to wear the seat belt? How about I just have her pin a note to my shirt next time that says 'He can sit up all by himself now?'"

We were at an impasse. He insisted I wear the seat belt, despite the fact that no one else was required to. I refused to comply and I was unwilling to get off the bus. Another bus had to be called out to deliver the other passengers to the car rental lot.

After a thirty-minute standoff, I got an idea. I transferred myself from my wheelchair into one of the seats on the bus. I smiled at the driver and said, "Now, what do you think? No seat belt over here." That was all it took to satisfy him, and he was willing to bring me to my car—unrestrained.

After my business trip, I wrote a letter to the company informing it that its policy of giving me less consideration than a toddler was offensive. I am certain that the policy did not come from a position of malice or intended prejudice. It was simply from making a stereotypical assumption—that I was incapable of making my own decisions regarding my own safety, while everyone else, toddlers included, were. The senior vice president of the company contacted me personally, apologized for the offense, and issued a policy change effective immediately.

I am sure that you have the same kind of daily challenges that take their toll and test your resolve over and over again. One of the most frequently asked questions I get from my audiences at speeches is, "How should we handle bad days?"

First, you must realize that although your bad day can seldom be anticipated, it only lasts for a short time. You should not make matters worse trying to convince yourself that a bad day is more than just that a bad DAY. I promise you, I could have used my travel experiences to make some dark, all-inclusive statement about how the world was out to make me feel miserable. People do have a tendency to take a bad-day experience and drag it out for days and weeks, making everyone around us miserable at the same time. But at times like this it's important to remember all the lessons I've been trying to pound into you about your ability to choose happiness. Choosing happiness, in large part, means consciously refusing to choose unhappiness.

I consider a bad day to be a lot like a cold virus. You usually catch it when you've been around a lot of other people who are sick, and there is often very little you can do about it. A doctor can sympathize with you. A spouse may try and pamper you. You can make all kinds of moaning sounds. But the reality is, it usually will last for twenty-four to forty-eight hours. The cure is the same today as it was when your mother nursed you back to health. Get some rest. Relax. And start again tomorrow.

Sound too simplistic? Perhaps. However, there is great power in the underlying principle. The idea is that everything is temporary. Think about it. A cold is temporary. A bad day is temporary. Sometimes the only solution to certain problems is the passing of time. The important thing is to not let a bad day become a bad week. Don't let a bad week become a bad year. And certainly don't make a bad year into a bad life.

One of the advantages I experienced from the beginning was that I viewed my circumstances as being temporary. Perhaps it came from being immature or naive, but I held to the hope that tomorrow things would change. At first, I naively held to the faith that somehow I would wake up tomorrow and all my problems would be solved. As each day passed, I realized that my condition would be much more long-term, and I had to prepare for that eventuality. However, I still never saw my circumstances as being permanent. That's significant. Don't forget this. Anytime you view your situation as permanent, you set yourself up for deeper disappointment and frustration.

The reality is: Everything is temporary. Success. Happiness. Wealth. Poverty. Failure. Sickness. Everything has an end. Success and happiness are not self-perpetuating. It takes focus, effort, and an adherence to lasting principles. Likewise, failure, sickness, and poverty are also not permanent; we can change our circumstances as soon as we are willing to change our behavior.

We have an epidemic of depression in this country. Communities are clamoring to have fluoride added to the water systems to cut down on cavities. We should probably explore a way of adding Prozac to the water, too. While I am not qualified to discuss the causes or merits of clinical depression, I can speak to the sense of depression every one of us has experienced from time to time when our conditions seem overwhelming. Some people have been mystified that, despite my obvious challenges, I have never described my emotional state as being depressed. Now, don't get me wrong; I have often been discouraged, frustrated, and cried myself to sleep at night. However, I don't know that I have ever been depressed. I think it will help if I describe my definition of depression: Discouragement without hope. Discouragement is a daily emotion for many people, me included. Discouragement evolves into depression, in my opinion, when we add the emotion of hopelessness. Depression sees everything as being permanent. Depression sees things as never changing. Depression sees no hope.

By taking the view that everything is temporary, what I am really saying is: There is always hope. Things change. Listen to your language. Do you use words like "never" and "always" a lot? *I will never be happy. It will always be this way. I am never appreciated. They always treat me like this. I never feel good.* Can you feel the sense of permanency and despair? The truth is, things are seldom "never and always." You are appreciated "sometimes." You have had moments when you felt good. The truth is: There is always hope. It starts with seeing our circumstances and conditions as being temporary. It's just a bad day. Go to bed and drink more fluids. Tomorrow will look better.

One other important thing you must learn—and I know I've been hammering this idea at you over and over throughout this book—is that you must not consume yourself with things that you cannot control. There is one obvious difference among people who are happy and successful versus those who are generally miserable and frustrated. Very often those who are unhappy are those whose conversations are centered around those things they cannot change. We all know how easy it is to complain about things we can't do anything about. It's easy. It passes the time. It doesn't require action. It doesn't require a solution. So we talk about the government, about the weather, about our parents, about our pasts.

Well, you can't overthrow the government, but you can work to get the right people running it. You can't change the weather, but you can always choose to stay inside. You can't change your parents, but you can work at being better parents yourself. You can't change your past, but you can make new choices today that will impact your future. And ultimately, though you can't control so many things in life, you can control how you respond. As I told you earlier, I used to be a fighter back in high school. I would get into fights with bigger guys and never give up, even when I knew there was no chance of winning. I thought I might be proving some point about my stubbornness or tenacity. The reality was that I was proving nothing. I was just getting one black eye after another. Today things aren't much different. I am still a fighter. The difference is, I pick my fights more carefully. I chose to do battle with the airline and the rental car company, for instance, because I believed that in those instances my battling would lead to a positive outcome. But other fights I let go. As much as I dislike the word "handicapped," I don't take the time to explain to people who call me handicapped why the word is offensive to me just because I happen to be in a wheelchair. I don't have the time to go on that particular crusade, and I also have learned that no matter what I say, people will still use that word.

One of the great breakthroughs that we can all make in life is not to get irritated over the little things that we cannot control.

Someone asked me, "Doesn't it drive you nuts to take so long to get dressed?" My answer was, "If I thought about it, it probably would. But I choose not to think about those things that I cannot control."

Think of all the frustrating events that take place in your life that you can do nothing about, and then think of how much easier your life would be if you responded to those events differently. Let's take an incident we're all familiar with: a traffic jam. It's a waste of our emotional energy to start slamming our hands on our steering wheels and blowing our horns and complaining about tied-up traffic. It won't get us anywhere any faster. So here's what I've learned do: I've learned not to think about traffic. Although I prefer not to be in the middle of a traffic tie-up, I force my mind to think about something else when it happens. I can't control the traffic, but I can choose how to respond to it. I choose not to be frustrated and angry. Consequently, I listen to a lot of talk radio.

Here's my last suggestion about getting over bad days: When you feel particularly afflicted, when you're caught up in your turmoil, a great way to restore a good feeling in yourself is not to focus on what you're going through, but to focus on doing something for someone else. When Dallas and I were first married, there were plenty of enormously frustrating days for me. We lived in a house that needed ramps for wheelchairs, wider doorways, doorknobs that would not be too difficult for my paralyzed hands to turn, extra room in the bathrooms and shower, and a much more open kitchen. It was difficult for me to do any of the things typically required of a man around the house. I couldn't mow the lawn, fix the dripping faucet, change the oil in the car, or move the heavy furniture for cleaning. What things I could do, I did. I picked things up around the house, even though it took me much longer than it would the average person. Sometimes I dragged the vacuum cleaner behind me around the carpet. I cleaned the kitchen, wiped the table, and tried to load the dishwasher. But sometimes the process of just getting dishes into the dishwasher was so hard that I would break dishes left and right and find myself physically tense with exasperation. By the time Dallas walked through the door after her own long day at the office, I wasn't exactly much fun to be around.

But then, after one frustrating day trying to maneuver around the house and get things done, I decided that I was going to respond differently. I rolled back into the kitchen, pulled food out of the refrigerator, and decided to cook Dallas a meal. I prepared a steak and baked potato dinner, complete with a tossed green salad. I dropped dishes, spilled food, and nearly chopped my fingers off trying to cut the potatoes. But because I was doing something for a person I loved, because I was focused more on the happiness of someone I cared for, I felt a fuller and deeper sense of happiness within myself.

FIFTEEN

❖

Balance Is Unachievable Until You Can Focus

STRATEGY: GIVE UP THE IDEA THAT YOU MUST HAVE
EVERYTHING IN YOUR LIFE THAT YOU WANT.
INSTEAD, FOCUS ON WHAT'S IMPORTANT.

I often get questions like, "Art, how do you do it all?" And my answer is, "Are you kidding? I can't do it all." The reality is that every day, I have to make choices. I choose to give some things up for other things. My desk, for instance, is always piled with paper because I have more ideas and to-do lists written down than I have time to do them. I have to make choices about what I need to do. I have to make choices among many appealing options, and sometimes those choices are painful. But as I do not hesitate to tell people, "All I can do is all I can do."

I know you hear a lot about "balance" these days. There are all sorts of books you can buy on creating a "balanced life." But I'm not sure balance is possible. If you were to put one foot in a bucket of boiling water and the other in a bucket of ice, on "average" you'd be just right—balanced. But you'd also be miserable. I don't think you can successfully devote equal amounts of time to so many facets of your life—your work, your home, your friends, your own needs. I've seen a lot of people so absorbed by so many tasks that they make surprisingly irrational demands on themselves. They don't know how or where to draw boundary lines, and as a result, they never feel that they are spending enough time in any area.

One of the challenges for many people today is that they have too many choices—good choices. When I was growing up we had about five TV channels to choose from; today, I have more than 200 via satellite. My first Internet connection in 1985 was at 300 bps; now I fly around the web at 1.5 megabits. When my father grew up, people worked at the same company for 40 years; when I grew up, it was hard to find someone who had changed jobs less than a half dozen times. Years ago, choosing a mate for life was generally restricted to your home town; in this modern age, you can marry through the Internet.

On one hand, the variety of choices is exciting. On the other hand, choices pose a challenge. Sometimes, because we have so many choices, we simply can't choose. People will spend hours flipping through their television channels because "there is nothing good to watch." The other problem with too many choices is that when we decide to pick something, we cannot forget that we are giving up something else. Often, we look longingly at what we have "given up" and wonder if we would be better off with a different choice.

In an interview, someone asked me, "How do you 'do it all'? You seem to be able to do everything. You have a successful career, rewarding business, loving family, three books, industry awards, public recognition, athletic skills, and time left over to play. How do you do it all?" The answer is, "I don't." Everyday I make choices. I do some things, I give up others. You should see my desk right now. It is piled high with papers, task lists, reports, books to read, and things to do. If I spent much time thinking about it, it would be overwhelming. So, I don't. I have several strategies for dealing with it.

First, every so often I take everything off my desk and stick it into a box and seal it with tape. I put the box into storage for thirty to ninety days and then I retrieve it. Now as I look through the box, 95 percent of it has become unimportant and irrelevant. And guess what? My life hasn't changed for the worse. The truth is, much of what we think is essential and urgent today has very little impact on the grand scheme of things.

Second, I remind myself of the title of a book I read some time ago, *All I Can Do Is All I Can Do, and That's Good Enough*. What a great idea. I can only do so much. I can't do everything. I must pick and choose. In the process, I must make sure that I choose the things that will ultimately make a difference. Now, I'll tell you how I choose.

Third, I attempt to follow the 80–20 rule for doing things that really matter. I try to spend 80 percent of my time doing things that I am uniquely qualified to do. For example, nobody else can be a father to my children or a husband to my wife. Nobody else can work out for me and take care of my body. Professionally, I am uniquely qualified to be a motivational speaker. Nobody can do that for me. On the other hand, there are lot of things I can do that I am not uniquely qualified for. These things tend to take away from my priorities. I am not particularly gifted at accounting, yard work, designing letterhead and web sites, or even opening mail. I have other people do these things. I know what some of you are thinking: "Well, wouldn't it be nice if I could afford to hire these things out, too?" True, these options require some financial resources. But I didn't start out this way. I began with little things. I had to draw the line somewhere. The most important thing you can do is to begin to make the distinctions between what you are uniquely qualified to do and that which you are not. Then, focus. It's also important to know that I make this same distinction for things other than my profession. For example, my wife is uniquely qualified to do many things, but one of her greatest strengths is being a mother to our children. Anything she is not uniquely qualified for simply detracts. As often as we are financially able, we hire out things like cleaning the garage, doing the ironing, and weeding the yard.

One day, when my son interrupted me doing my work with a question, I felt frustrated because of the interruption. Later I had to remind myself that my children are not an interruption to my work, my work is an interruption to my children. It starts with perspective and focus.

Balance begins with focus. Too often our minds are somewhere else. When we are at work, we wish we are at home. When we're at home, we wish we were on vacation. When we are on vacation, we take our work! What is happening is that you are often not being "present" with your friends or your children, even when you are with them, because your mind is so cluttered with everything else going on in your life. Your self-created fragmentation of your mind makes it difficult for you to do anything very well.

Often I ask people to tell me about all the improvements they want to make in their life, and they give me a grocery list of things they want to do or change. But if you are one of those who maintains fifty problems in your life and then go about trying to change everything, you will only meet with frustration and failure. Many people protect themselves from change by setting up so many seemingly important things to change that they always feel overwhelmed and never can get themselves together enough to do anything. They say things such as "I wouldn't know where to begin," or "Oh, I have so many problems, I could never work on just one at a time."

But what if they decided to zero in on one really important aspect of their life or their behavior that they wanted to change? And what if they gave this one issue their complete conscious attention, instead of worrying at the same time about other behaviors and feelings? Doing too many things, I have realized, reduces us to mediocrity in a lot of little things.

Here's what becoming a quadriplegic did for me—which is a lesson everyone could benefit from. After my accident, many choices were obviously taken away. But there was an advantage to that. With fewer choices, I have had fewer distractions. Brian Holloway, a great friend of mine, played football for the New England Patriots and Los Angeles Raiders. He was named to the Pro Bowl for five years and won a Super Bowl ring. Recently, he asked me what I do to work out, especially given all of my traveling. Well, I said, as a quadriplegic, I have a lot of advantages when it comes to working out. For instance, when only 20 percent of your body works, it takes 80 percent less time to train. It is easier for me to focus on the few muscles that work, rather than having to work out my entire body.

As a result, I didn't have to choose between whether I wanted to emphasize my thighs in my workout or my shoulders; my shoulders were all I had. I didn't have to choose how to use my discretionary time between golf and racquetball; I was barely mastering pushing myself down the street.

With fewer choices, I didn't have the luxury of second-guess-ing my choices or thinking that "the grass was greener on the other side of the fence." I had no choice but to utilize the opportunities I had. I had to make those opportunities work. I learned to focus.

You already know that there is a tremendous power in focus, in that laser beam of awareness. You know what happens when you focus your mind on one subject to the exclusion of everything else. It's like completing your tax returns before midnight on April 15th. Your mind is sharper. You're far less likely to be distracted.

Instead of trying to make your life better by being "balanced"— making yourself, for instance, spend eight hours at work, eight hours at home, eight hours asleep—you'd be better off learning to choose what's really important to you, then focusing on those things. Your "balance" will then take care of itself.

Because of the professional success I've had as a speaker, I deliver more than 150 speeches a year. That means I'm traveling nearly six months of every year. Yet none of that success can replace the time and energy I spend with my wife and two delight-ful children, whom I adore. The greatest achievement I will ever aspire to will be found within the walls of my home and in the lives of my children. As David O'McKay, a prominent religious leader in 1954, stated, "No success can compensate for failure in the home." So the question for me is, "How can I fulfill my desire to be a speaker and fulfill my other desire to be the most loving husband and father?" Even though the bad news is that I travel so often, the good news is that I am home more than six months of the year. And I make sure that when I am at home, I am at home. Thus, when I'm on the road, I carry a laptop with me to answer correspondence, return e-mails, plan strategy, write, and do research. I rarely eat an in-flight meal, because that is forty-five minutes to get more work done. The more I achieve on the road and the better I utilize my time, the more easily I can focus exclusively on my family when I come through the front door. This keeps me highly motivated.

When I am on the road, I also stay in constant contact with my family through phone calls, e-mail, postcards, and live streaming video. I take a digital camera on the road with me to take pictures of things my children would be interested in and e-mail them home. My children, likewise, have their own digital camera and can take pictures of things of interest to them and e-mail their pictures back. Before I leave, I discuss with my children where I am going and what is unique about those areas: Boston for its crabs. Seattle for its salmon. Louisiana for its Cajun food. And, of course, Orlando for Mickey Mouse. Once a month, my wife, Dallas, picks a city of interest and travels with me for a couple of days while the children spend time with their grandparents. Once every three months, we take the whole family and stay for a week in such places as Hawaii, Bermuda, Atlanta, Orlando, and the Bahamas. As my children are getting older, I am beginning to take them individually with me on the road to a variety of cities for a special "date with Dad."

While at home, my goal is to go into the office only when my children are in school. (My office is attached to my home, with a separate outside entrance for employees, so my entire commute takes only nine seconds. There's never a traffic jam.) And when I'm in that office, I work, and then at the end of the day, I do everything I can to leave work at work, even though it's a mere nine seconds away.

As I explained earlier, when it comes to my life, I live by what I call the "80–20" rule. I try to spend 80 percent of my time doing what I think I am uniquely qualified to do. That means 80 percent of my time is devoted to being a father and a husband and to my career as a public speaker. The other 20 percent of my time I devote to hobbies or whatever it is that happens to interest me. I like, for instance, to design web pages. I'm not very good at it, but it's fun. However, I don't let it take much time out of my day because that's not what I'm uniquely qualified to do.

By learning to focus your mind, you'll find yourself staying far more motivated to achieve whatever it is you want to achieve. As you do not have to be told, staying "motivated" is tricky business. I was once sitting on a plane, flying back from a speaking engagement in Orlando. The passenger seated next to me was the kind you always dread as a frequent flier. He wanted to talk. Although I had a lot of work to do —letters to write, e-mail to respond to, and correspondence to read—the passenger was determined to talk to me as long as he could.

"Where are you going?" he inquired. "Home," was my response. "Where's home?" he continued. "Utah," was my answer. "What do you do for a living?" he pressed. "I am a motivational speaker," I replied.

There was a pause. "You sure don't look very motivated right now," he offered.

That got me thinking. Just what does "motivated" look like? What does it feel like? Was I supposed to be energetic, bubbly, jumping up and down with the energy of a child? What do people expect from a "motivated" person?

Consider for a moment the way I looked on that plane. I wasn't peppy the way you expect a motivational speaker to be. I wasn't outgoing and exuberant. The fact that I was not "social" to a fellow passenger might have suggested that I was unmotivated in some way.

In truth, I was very motivated at that moment. I was focused. I knew that the more work I could get done while I was on the road, the more time I would have to spend with my children at home. Sure, I could have kicked back, swapped stories, thrown out a few aphorisms. But I was working. I was focused—which is true motivation.

I recall my father telling me the story of an older man who had trouble with some of the younger kids in his neighborhood. Every day, a group of teenagers would come by his home and throw rocks at it. The old man did everything he could to stop the mischievous boys from throwing those rocks. He called the police, called the boys' parents, and shouted threats at the boys from his porch. Nothing he did seemed to stop their behavior. In contrast, the young men seemed more encouraged than ever to keep throwing.

In desperation, the old man met with the boys and struck a deal. "Boys, I want you to know I've changed my mind about how I've been feeling," he said. "I have come to enjoy you throwing rocks at my home. For that reason, I am willing to pay each of you a dollar every day that you throw rocks at my house." Although bewildered, the boys enthusiastically agreed and began to show up each day at the appointed time to throw the rocks. As understood, the old man happily paid them a dollar each. This went on for a few days, and then the old man approached the boys and said, "I have been having some financial troubles lately and I can no longer afford to pay you each a dollar. Would you be willing to consider fifty cents?" After conferring with each other, the boys reluctantly agreed to keep throwing rocks at his house for just fifty cents each.

Then another few days went by before the old man approached the boys with more bad news. "Boys, I have really fallen on some financial hard times. I cannot afford to pay you fifty cents a day. However, I could still pay you each a dime for throwing the rocks." The boys exchanged glances and then one of them abruptly said, "There is no way we are going to throw rocks at your house for only a dime apiece." And with that, they left and never came back.

What happened? Before, the boys were willing to throw rocks for nothing. They were "internally" motivated by the sense of adventure, variety, bonding, element of risk, and desire to belong. When they began accepting money for throwing rocks, their motivation slowly shifted to external sources—financial reward. In a short time, they forgot why they ever did it to begin with. When the financial rewards were eliminated, their motivation was gone.

Are you driven by internal or external motivation? If the majority of your motivation is from external sources, you will find it hard to sustain, especially in difficult times. But if you're internally motivated, then you'll put off the pleasures of the moment for something more valuable. You'll do what you should be doing rather than always what you want to be doing. You'll focus on what's important in the face of other distractions.

Let me be very honest with you: You will always be able to build up a short-term burst of energy that will lead to some change. If you need to lose weight so you'll look good for a wedding in two weeks, you can do it. If you have a major project that must be completed by a certain tight deadline—or else you lose your job—you'll figure out how to get it done. All of us can find some sort of leverage to get things done in the moment. We have a certain amount of willpower. But this is so important for you to understand: Willpower is never going to be enough. It never works over a very long period of time. So many people come to one of my speeches hoping that I can increase their willpower or instantly motivate them, as if I am a magician. They think I am some kind of cheerleader who can pump them up long enough for them to get a particular task accomplished, like increasing their sales or getting promoted or building a new business, or improving a relationship or enhancing their family life.

What I tell them is that if they want to accomplish that task, they need to be focused, and they need time. They shouldn't worry about how long it takes to accomplish something: It takes as long as it takes. Let me use myself as an example. It wasn't being born with a special gift of gab that made me a well-regarded, financially successful speaker. It was spending years listening to audiotapes of the masters of oratory—countless hours of the world's top speakers at their best. I then spoke for free more than 500 times over the course of seven years. I was willing to make an investment of time and focus to become a professional. There. That's it. I am not sure the formula for success is much different for any true professional, regardless of their vocation.

What does motivation look like? Well, it doesn't have anything to do with what you look like. It's all about what you do when you are focused. It is the individual who quietly goes about his work, doing his duty, without the need for constant reassurance or praise. It is someone who does what he or she should be doing every day when it would be so easy to get diverted and do something more relaxing. It is the teenager who studies late into the night when he could have been doing something more fun. It's the politician who lobbies for causes that will have real impact and meaning as opposed to those things that are politically expedient and popular.

How can you tell if you're motivated? Ask yourself some of these questions:

- Do you avoid the difficult things in pursuit of the "busy" things?
- Do you focus on long-term goals or just short-term pleasure?
- Do you put off pleasure when more important work needs to be done?
- Do you know what you should do, or what you just want to do?

I wish I could put this in a gentler way, but the plain truth is that all the self-understanding that might have come to you since you started reading this book will be pointless if you do not learn how to focus on the tasks you set before yourself. As idealistic as you are about changing your life, no change will come to you without focus, without constant awareness.

And here is one more truth I cannot put more gently: You are not born with focus. It is something you have to train yourself to do every day. You have to concentrate like you've never concentrated before. But it can become a powerful habit—a gradual and steady conditioning of the mind.

This is not an abstract concept. It is not a silly, pie-in-the-sky theory. It is a significant factor in determining who succeeds and who fails. To get their minds focused, for instance, professional performers go so far as to mentally rehearse their performances before they go on. The night before a surgery, Dr. Charles Mayo, the founder of the Mayo Clinic, would mentally rehearse everything he was going to do, from putting on his surgical garb to making his first incision. The members of the U.S. women's gymnastics team who won the 1996 Olympic gold medal were taught to "visualize" their entire routines prior to competing.

Perhaps you have heard the story of Liu Chi Kung, China's premier concert pianist, who was imprisoned in 1959 during the political revolution in China. Liu Chi Kung's arrest was devastating news to the international arts community because only a year earlier, he had placed second in the international Van Cliburn Competition. He was held for seven years, during which he was never allowed to touch a piano. When Liu Chi Kung was released, people assumed he would never regain his ability. But within a year of his freedom, he gave a concert tour—and the stunned critics said he was better than he was before he went to prison. How did he do it? The musician said that in his jail cell, he practiced every single day—in his mind! He rehearsed all his repertoire, over and over. He was able to focus his mind so intently that he might as well have been at a keyboard.

During a visit several years ago to a medical meeting in Italy, Dr. Charles Garfield, a clinical professor at the UCLA School of Medicine, began listening to some European scientists who had spent millions of dollars on research on how to train athletes for optimum performance. When they began talking about the power of focus, Garfield was skeptical. So they asked him to participate in a research experiment. They took him to a gym, hooked him up to monitors that measured brain waves, heartbeat, and muscle tension, and then asked him to attempt to bench-press as much as he could.

Under enormous strain, Dr. Garfield raised 300 pounds of weight. He said he might be able, if he was lucky, to lift ten pounds more—but that was it. The scientists, however, asked Garfield to relax, breathe deeply, and imagine lifting not just ten pounds more, but twenty pounds more. For more than thirty minutes, they had him focus on the image of grabbing the bar and successfully pushing it up. After several mental rehearsals, they put him back down on the bench and asked him to lift the barbell above him. Garfield, his mind totally focused, lifted the barbell easily.

But here's the catch. The weight wasn't just 310 pounds. It was 365 pounds! And the scientists were certain they could get him to 400 pounds. All this from a man who was mostly out of shape!

Garfield became so convinced of the power of a focused mind that he began to research the topic himself when he returned to the United States. He found that most high achievers in American business intensely focus their thoughts. "They see in their mind's eye the result they want, and the actions leading to it," Garfield wrote.

Are you getting the picture? Motivation isn't just saying, "I can do this! I can achieve!" It's focusing. It's getting an image of what you want to be in your mind, and then concentrating diligently and working ceaselessly until that image comes true.

SIXTEEN

✳

When We're Laughing, We're Learning

STRATEGY: LAUGHTER IS ESSENTIAL TO CREATIVITY,
INNOVATION, AND PERSPECTIVE.
EVEN THE MOST SERIOUS CAN
LEARN TO LAUGH AND PLAY MORE.

One of the best ways to avoid overdramatizing one's fears, as well as to avoid the misconception that our problems are permanent, is to laugh at them. Just throw your head back and laugh in the face of fear, and in the midst of struggle. Life is serious enough without you having to be so serious about it.

The reason laughter, play, and even frivolity are so good for the soul is that we overestimate the pain we think we are feeling, especially during times of adversity. Even when life seems at its darkest or most difficult, there is immense therapeutic value in chuckling at what you're having to go through. There is also value in "play," which is a physical release for your inner turmoil or anxiety. The role of "play" is often underestimated. What do I mean by this? Read the following stories to see if you can get a better idea.

One of the first things I had to deal with after my accident was the inevitable difficulty of getting around in a wheelchair. I could have remained permanently embarrassed by the times I spilled out of that wheelchair and needed help back in, or all the times I had lost control of the wheelchair. I could have become consumed with the way people do double-takes when they see me. There is a certain friend whose apartment makes it hard to visit because to enter his building, you have to walk downstairs a dozen steps. If I'm going to get down there, I need two people to help me, one grabbing the front of my wheelchair and the other the back. But I've made the decision that the way to handle the uncomfortable moments is to laugh about them. One night when I visited, my brother was at the back of the chair, and a friend held the front. Before the effort began, I gave precise instructions, in a mock, comic voice, of the responsibilities of each carrier. "The job of the man in the back is to bear most of the weight, set the pace as we go, and make a covenant to never let go," I explained. "The man up front has one principle responsibility—in the event that the man in back is unfaithful and drops the chair with me in it, the front man is to sacrifice his body in an effort to save me! Are we understood?"

Both men responded reassuringly, but no sooner had we begun the descent when my brother slipped on a step and began to fall forward. The friend, seeing me and my wheelchair falling toward him, instinctively jumped clear of our path. Uh-oh. Falling, rolling, bumping, banging, I made my way ungracefully to the bottom, my brother still clinging desperately to the chair as he fell behind me. Luckily, we only received minor bumps and bruises.

On another occasion, trying to prove my independence, I decided to go shopping by myself at a mall that was three stories high with more than 200 stores. At one point, I was on the third level and wanting to go down to the second level. The mall contained long sloping ramps that connected the floors, and as I sat at the top of that great abyss and looked down into the valley below, I decided I could manage those ramps. I waited for a crowd to move, and then I pushed off.

An interesting thing happened when I pushed off. I accelerated. I mean, really accelerated. Because I don't have the use of my hands, I could only put some outside pressure on my wheels. I did what I could, but I kept going faster and faster. After a few seconds, I began to smell burning flesh coming from my hands, and I knew I was in trouble.

Being the good Boy Scout that I was, I was obviously more concerned for the safety of young mothers and their children at the bottom of the ramp than I was for myself. After all, what more can you do to hurt a quadriplegic? What am I going to do, break my neck? So I began to wave my arms and shout, "Get out of the way, get out of the way!" Mothers ran to the right, children to the left.

Then I noticed another interesting thing happening as I waved my arms. I accelerated even more. I hit the bottom of that ramp at full speed. I'm not sure how fast I was going—it felt like 80, 90, 100 miles an hour. Whatever it was, I was racing right through the middle of all those good mall shoppers and began heading for a store in front of me. The name across the front of the store was A. Hurst & Sons Jewelers. In that split second, I realized that I was about to reenact the classic "bull in a china shop" scene. But this bull was going at full speed. I had a feeling I was about to teach them a new meaning of the word "layaway." I raced right down through the middle of that store and I kept waving my arms and shouting, "Get out of the way." More people ran to the right, more to the left. Salespeople were jumping over the counters and hiding behind pedestals. The man who looked most worried was the man in the very back. He was the man behind the repair counter. He had a look on his face as if he could sense we were going to get very well acquainted.

On that day, however, I was a lucky man. There was carpeting on the floor with thick padding underneath. I began to slow down, and I came to a stop right in front of the repair counter. The repairman looked down over the counter, paused, and said, "Can I help you?"

I paused, too, then said, "Yes, sir, can you tell me what time it is? I'm in an awful hurry."

That ill-fated trip didn't end my visits to the mall. Dallas always loved me to go shopping with her because I made a great shopping cart. One day she told me she had to run to the mall to get a couple of items. I came along, and while she headed for the department store, I slipped into one of my favorite places—a bookstore. Since it was almost closing time, I told Dallas she could easily find me among the books when she was finished. She hurried off.

I spent the next few minutes searching through titles in the back of the store. Soon I heard Dallas's footsteps coming up the long aisle. From the months in the hospital, I had learned to recognize the sound of her distinct walk. Almost without thinking, I hid behind a bookshelf as she walked past. She hadn't seen me. This was going to be fun, I thought.

Reaching the back of the store and not finding me, she turned and started back. I hid again, this time in the mystery section. She walked past. Knowing that if I hid for too long she might get worried, I decided to give away my hiding place by whistling at her. Dallas and I often whistled at one another as a show of affection.

I whistled just loud enough for her to hear. The footsteps hesitated, stopped, and then began again toward the rear of the store. Not wanting to make this too easy, I slid behind another shelf of books as she walked right by. I chuckled to myself as I considered my advantage. With the hunt now well in progress, I whistled affectionately again, only this time louder. The footsteps began toward me, quicker than before. I slid behind a different set of shelves. She walked right past. This was too easy. It never took Dallas this long to figure out what I was doing. She was headed for the front of the store again.

This is ridiculous, I thought. I'd give her one last chance before I surrendered. I whistled that affectionate tune again, as loud as I could. The footsteps stopped, paused a moment, and then quickly continued. I was confused. I concluded that I should give myself up. I pulled into the open aisle. "Hi, sweetheart," I shouted, "I'm over here." The blonde hair swung around. "I'm sorry, sir," said the woman, "but we're closing."

It wasn't Dallas! It was the manager of the store. My face turned about fifty different shades of red as I said, "Thank you, I was leaving anyway."

There is healing power in laughter. It makes us forget, makes us relax, and makes us feel like life is worth living again. When a person inhibits himself from allowing the full expression of his emotions, he poisons himself.

One of the greatest aspects of being alive is play. Without exception, people need play. People whose lives are lopsided with work have a lack of appreciation for play. Thinking their lives are "serious business," they give up play too readily. They think they cannot afford time away from work and chores. Instead, they grind away, insisting that staying alive means work and rest in an unending cycle. If only they could read the words of Plato: "Watch a man play for an hour and you can learn more about him than in talking to him for a year."

As you might remember, the doctors told me to forget about sports. Their idea for me, apparently, was to watch sports on TV.

I said to myself, "Forget it." As I got stronger, I started snow skiing on a sled-like ski with short poles in my hands (we call it "sit-skiing"). I relearned to play tennis and relearned to swim. Or as my family says, I learned to swim like a rock. (At least I learned to hold my breath really well.) It didn't matter. And then there was my attempt to scuba dive. I tried it with my family while we were vacationing in Hawaii. I had never tried it before, and it was hard to imagine that I was going to enjoy it. But my brother said he was going to throw me in the ocean anyway, and he just thought a little oxygen would be nice to help me get by. I finally agreed. I went through all the instruction: the safety training and education and the technique of diving. Finally the time came to dive into the ocean. I put on the wet suit on, then had the air tank strapped to my back, the buoyancy compensator vest put around my chest, and the weight belt around my waist. Then they put the little flippers on my feet. (I'm not sure why they thought the flippers would help, since I couldn't move my feet. But they looked really good.)

As they were dragging me into the water, I overheard one of my brothers say that I looked like shark bait. I was getting a much better idea of why I had been invited. With my buoyancy compensator vest, I could rise or drop in the water, depending on how much air I let in or out of that jacket. With my jacket full, I could float on the surface looking at the ocean floor. I was extremely comfortable. But the instructor had a whole new plan for my future. (Have you ever had that experience at work before? You were comfortable doing what you were doing, happy with your life, then someone had a plan?) The instructor came up, and he let all the air out of my jacket. I began to descend in the water. But there was only one problem with my descent. With the flippers on my feet, my feet tended to float toward the surface—far more than my head. Then, with more air let out of my vest, I went straight down to the bottom, fifty feet down, and I hit my head on the bottom of the ocean floor. My flippers were sticking straight up above me. Even the fish were giving me strange looks. The instructor, eager to help, came down beside me and let all the air back into my jacket. And just like that, I went straight back up again, feet first, passing my family on the way. My feet surfaced at the top, kind of like the submarine in *The Hunt for Red October.*

My instructor thought if I took my weight belt off of my waist and put it around my knees, perhaps I would float flatter in the water instead of having my feet bobbing above the surface with my head still pointing to the ocean floor. The idea might have worked, except the belt started slipping down around my ankles—and back to the bottom of the ocean I went. There I remained for a few minutes, waving at my family, as they waved curiously back. They were compassionate. From time to time they would return, pick me off my rock, and stick me on a new one.

But my Jacques Cousteau act was nothing compared to my decision to join a wheelchair rugby team. Thirty-two minutes of hell: that is how wheelchair rugby is often described. It originated in Canada in 1980 and was originally called "murder ball"—a name that didn't quite lend itself to corporate sponsors. Later the name was changed to wheelchair rugby or quad rugby (because the game itself is restricted to quadriplegics). Today there are more than 70 teams in the United States and another 40 abroad. It is one of the fastest-growing wheelchair sports in the world. Wheelchair rugby is played on a basketball court with a volleyball. There are two teams, each consisting of four players in wheelchairs. The object of the game is to get the ball across a goal line (which is 24 feet wide at the other end of the court). To get the ball there, you can roll it, throw it, bounce it, or pass it to another team member, who can then try to get the ball across. However, a player must have control of the ball when he or she crosses the goal line for it to be considered a score. Those who have not watched the game have missed a unique form of athletics. With total disregard to what they can or cannot do, athletes race from one end of the court to the other, bumping, colliding, grabbing, swinging, and picking (as they'd say in basketball). When eight quadriplegics of varying classifications are let loose on one court, there is no such word as "quit." Our motto in rugby is that "the hit isn't real unless it bends steel."

During one exhibition match with another team, it was my job to watch the left side of the goal line—to keep out both the players and the ball. The other team's strategy was to send all four players at the goal line as fast as they could. The point man, realizing that we couldn't block the entire line altogether, would pass the ball at the last minute to the player with the best opportunity. Upon catching and keeping the ball, the player's speed and momentum alone would carry him across the goal line.

We were all caught up in the vigor and competitive spirit of the game. My pulse quickened in the final moment as the ball came to my side. However, the ball was just outside the reach of my opponent. As he stretched his arms and torso to pull the ball into his lap, his chair went up onto just two wheels, leaving him off-center and unbalanced. I knew if he righted himself, got the ball, and maintained control, his speed and momentum would carry him victoriously across the goal line. There seemed to be only one solution: I pushed him over.

Now don't worry too much about the other guy. He wasn't hurt much. He cut his leg a bit, but he couldn't feel it anyway! I guess it was fair for them to throw me into the penalty box for a couple of minutes. Later, I had a good laugh with the athlete I had pushed. To be honest, it thrilled us to be involved again in a competitive game that didn't protect us from hard knocks. To feel our muscles work and fight again, even in their limited way, was more satisfying than any of us could express. We felt alive and invigorated while pushing, maneuvering, and playing, doing the very things our doctors and therapists said we would not be doing. In fact, our little wheelchair rugby team from Utah eventually was ranked sixteenth in the nation.

One of the problems with my love of sports is that my body doesn't sweat anymore. Such a condition does have its advantages: I have saved a bundle of money on deodorant. However, not being able to sweat, which is the body's natural mechanism for cooling off, means that my body temperature quickly rises with the outside temperature. While engaged in active sports or when exposed for too long to high outside temperatures, my body can dangerously heat up, bringing the possibility of heatstroke, and even death. My breathing gets labored and heavy, my eyes turn glossy, my head becomes light, and my body becomes extremely weak.

One hot summer afternoon when I was still living in San Jose, California, outside temperatures rose to a sweltering 107 degrees, and the air conditioning broke inside our home. For three hours I wore a path in the carpet between the cool running water of the bathroom sink and the fan whirring at high speed. I would completely soak my head under the cold water and then sit directly in front of the fan. Nevertheless, after three hours, my body temperature continued to rise and I began to suffer the danger signs.

Time was not on my side as the minutes ticked by. I finally pushed myself outside, got into my van, and headed for one place I knew I could find ultimate relief: the grocery store. Wheeling weakly through the automatic doors, I felt the rush of environmentally controlled cool air whisper across my face and neck. But

for me that wasn't enough. I wheeled toward the frozen food section, pulled the glass doors open, and laid my head right down on
the frozen corn. Ahhhhh! I could have lived there all day if it
wasn't for shoppers beginning to look at me and make curious
comments. Fearing I would discourage frozen corn sales, I left my
bastion of comfort and made my way to another source of relief,
the meat department. Finding the butcher, I announced, "I'm in
serious trouble, and need to cool down fast, sir. May I please sit in
your meat freezer?" With a puzzled look, he gestured for me to follow as we entered through a doorway of mist and escaping cold
air. Finally, sitting alongside frozen sides of beef and with my
breath showing in the crisp air, the effects of the heat began to
diminish.

However, only minutes later, the butcher returned and apolo-
getically responded, "I'm sorry, sir, but I am afraid that if I leave
you in here much longer you'll end up looking like one of the sides
of beef. That would not reflect well on my job. But if you'll follow
me, I have a better solution."

Moments later I sat in the cool air of the dairy locker behind
rows of milk, cottage cheese, and yogurt. I figured that as long as I
was here, I might as well have some fun. As shoppers reached
their hands toward the yogurt, they heard a voice, distinct and
commanding: "Don't buy the strawberry. Get me, the vanilla!"
Shoppers looked hesitantly to the right and left, and then stared
into the rows of yogurt trying to find the source of the voice they
were sure they heard. Mystery unsolved, they nervously loaded
their carts with vanilla yogurt.

Perhaps you're thinking, "Well, these stories were entertaining,
but what do I learn from them?" Here's what you learn from them:
When we're laughing, I think we're learning. It opens our minds

up and makes us more creative and innovative. It helps us to view our challenges from a unique perspective. When you laugh and you play, you are having that moment-to-moment experience of you at your best. When you laugh and play, your body releases endorphins, the chemicals that produce feelings of well-being, happiness, and contentment. Doing such activities is a gift to yourself. You're nurturing yourself with the same passion with which you nurture anything or anyone you love. You're giving yourself the chance to live your life out loud.

SEVENTEEN

❋

Remember That Some Miracles Take Time

STRATEGY: REDISCOVER YOUR CHILDLIKE
SENSE OF WONDERMENT ABOUT LIFE.
SUCH A QUALITY WILL GET YOU THROUGH
EVEN THE ROUGHEST OF TIMES.

Some time ago I was involved in a business relationship that became an enormous burden because of illegal activities by one of the parties. I had been treated dishonorably, and it was costing me financially and emotionally.

Before long, attorneys were being introduced into the embroiled relationship. Harsher words were being spoken, threats made, and battle plans detailed for a lengthy legal confrontation. I was spending tens of thousands of dollars in legal fees, for no other reason than to protect my good name, which I had done nothing to besmirch. I was tempted to go back to why-ning, asking why I had been doing so well and yet this other part of my life was coming apart at the seams. Despite my strong belief that "nothing bad ever happens without an equal or greater benefit coming in return," I was struggling to keep my hopes and dreams alive.

Then late one night I received a phone call from the attorney I had hired. I sighed when I heard his voice, thinking we were going to have to talk about an upcoming legal deposition. But to my complete surprise, he said, "Art, have you and Dallas considered adopting children?"

I was taken aback. For two years, Dallas had tried unsuccessfully to have children. We had talked about adoption but decided against it because of the time, money, and stress involved. I told the lawyer that we had concluded it would be more productive to spend our efforts attempting to bear our own children.

"Well, Art, I just want you to know, besides business law, I have done a number of adoptions," the attorney said. "And it just happens that I know of a fifteen-month-old girl who's available right now."

"Right now?"

"There's a waiting list of potential parents already," he said, "but for some reason, Art, I feel compelled to call you and give you the first opportunity to adopt her."

Within forty-eight hours—forty-eight hours!—a little girl came to our home. Her name was McKenzie. She was our new daughter. As I said, nothing bad ever happens without an equal or greater benefit coming in return. If the painful legal confrontation had never commenced, McKenzie would never have found her way to our home.

The minute she came into our house, I could not imagine life without her. It was as if McKenzie had always been meant to be part of our family—she had just taken a different route to get there.

Children do change your life. Anyone who's even been around children understands the difference they can make. That was certainly true for Dallas and me. When McKenzie came into our lives, it changed everything. We worked overtime to make a loving place for her. We embraced her, told her stories, tried to make her feel reassured. Even though she was only fifteen months old, I'm sure this was a difficult and confusing time for her, but as the days passed, she began accepting our blankets of love. Soon we began to see the real McKenzie. Her eyes danced with curiosity. Her smile lit up a room. Her love was infectious. Everyone wanted to be her friend.

We then, amazingly, were given the opportunity to adopt another child. A friend put us in touch with a young, unwed mother-to-be. While her pregnancy was due to what she called a lapse of judgment on her part, she was not willing to abandon the life that was growing inside her. Dallas and I will be eternally grateful for her decision, for it allowed us to be given the wonderful gift of a son. We named him Dalton. Under a partially open adoption agreement, we brought him home from the hospital three days after he was born. From the beginning, he had some health challenges—a strain of pneumonia, colic, and jaundice. For two weeks, he had to sleep in a special incubator with needles stuck in his little arm and tubes taped to his wrist. It was heartbreaking to watch. However, in the days that we watched over him, prayed for him, and hoped for him, our love grew immeasurably.

I love to talk about my children because many of the greatest lessons in my life I have learned directly from them. My children, for instance, do not consider important what anyone "does for a living" or what fancy material props they have to distinguish themselves. To them, everyone is unique and wondrous. Everyone has a kind of divine spark, a very valuable inner core.

My children also have taught me about the importance of resilience in this world. I am convinced that there are times when my children have never heard me say the word, "No." Oh, I've said it—many, many times. I am just not sure they have ever heard it. To a child, "No" means "maybe." Or it means, "You should ask your other parent." Or it means, "I just need to rephrase my question." Or it means, "It's still early in the day. I can still wear you down."

You can go so far as to say to a child, "My final answer is no, no, no," and they will wander off to their room, draw you a picture, and write across the bottom, "I love you, Daddy." Do you have one of those on your refrigerator? It's because children intuitively understand that when faced with frustration, rejection, and change, they only need to love, serve, and give a little more.

What's more, children are willing to risk failure to achieve. Just watch children learn to walk. Before they finally take their first steps, they fall down a hundred times, looking ridiculous each time they crash. If they cared about how ridiculous they looked, then they would quit trying and never learn to walk. But to them, they are not failing. Oh, if we could just have that sense of determination.

One afternoon Dalton was playing his favorite music from his CD player as loudly as he could. I was able to hear the music from the other end of the house. When I finally found Dalton, I asked him, "Don't you think the music is too loud?"

"Oh, no, Dad, it's not too loud," Dalton exclaimed confidently.

Trying to persuade him, I said, "Don't you think the neighbors will get mad?"

"Oh, no, Dad, they get to hear it, too."

How would things change for you if you could see things through the eyes of a child? Children have a natural tendency to share and to want others to have what they have. They assume the best in people, and they often give us the benefit of the doubt.

Dallas was driving the kids to school recently. At a traffic light, a car full of teenage boys flashed a hand-lettered sign to my wife saying, "Will you go out with me?" Taking advantage of a teaching moment, Dallas explained to our children that the boys were acting inappropriately. McKenzie, figuring she had grasped the whole lesson, exclaimed, "Yes, Mom, I think they are being very rude. They should have said, 'Will you go out with me *tonight*?' "

Children don't read other things into our messages. They hear what we say exactly as we say it. They don't assume prejudice, malice, or politics.

I asked one night when Dalton was in a particularly adorable mood, "How come you are so cute?"

"I don't know," he replied shyly.

"Is it because your mom is a babe?" I asked him, smiling.

Dalton gave me a bewildered look and asked, "Mommy is a pig?"

I realized the kids had just watched the movie *Babe* and all Dalton could relate to was that "babe" was a talking pig. I quickly told him that Mom was not a pig and that if he repeated the story to his mother, I'd deny it.

Children also should remind us of the importance of being naturally curious and inquisitive. They question everything, not to defy authority as much as to expand their knowledge. I'll never forget a conversation that McKenzie, then six, and Dalton, then three, once had about change. My daughter turned to my son and said, "When I grow up, I'm going to be a mom." My son, not wanting to be outdone, said, "I'm going to be a mom, too." McKenzie indignantly replied, "You can't be a mom, you can only be a dad." Just as indignantly, Dalton said, "I don't want to be a dad, I want to be a mom."

"No," exclaimed McKenzie. "You can only be a dad." My son got a little teary-eyed, and he said, "I don't want to be a dad, I want to be a mom." Finally, my daughter leaned over and patted Dalton on the knee and she said, "Dalton, you can't change it, so just accept it."

How much more could we learn if we approached our work and challenges the same way? In an environment of change we need to look at things from a different perspective. We need to challenge old ways of thinking and doing to remain competitive and vital. Our challenges should come not from our pride and ego, but from our curiosity and willingness to do new things.

As my children have grown up I have tried to teach them correct principles. Among other things I thought that they should know was that as their father, I knew everything! This philosophy worked well for the first few years. When they asked how I knew something, my answer was simple and direct. "As your father, I know everything."

I thought I could carry on this charade for a good while until Dalton challenged my knowledge one day by asking, "Dad, how do you know that?" Without missing a beat I responded, as I always had for the first five years of his life, "Dalton, as your dad, I know everything." He put his little hands on his hips and said defiantly, "Dad, you don't know everything. Only Jesus and Santa know everything." I couldn't stop laughing. And then I thought, "Well, at least I'm Santa. I can live with that."

They also can teach us about the joy that comes from helping others. A few years ago, my daughter came home from school very excited because someone had taught her to do a thumbs-up sign. She was told that when you give someone a thumbs up, that means you've done something exceptionally well—something that should make you proud.

She asked me to do it. I tried, but with the limited use of my hands, my thumb just stayed flat. That was as good as it got. I tried to explain to her that it wasn't from a lack of desire—it was just gravity. For a six-year-old little girl, at the time, that was okay.

A few weeks after that experience, McKenzie was at a dance recital with some friends of hers. My wife and I were both there to watch. She was so cute and adorable, and as her father I couldn't have been more proud. In a brief moment, as our eyes made contact, I gave her my "flat" version of the thumbs-up. When she saw me, she suddenly ran from her little dance group out into the audience. She came over to my side and held my thumb up. And then she said, "There you go, Daddy. Now I can help."

Do you have the ability, willingness, and desire to help others? Are you willing to give others a "thumbs-up" for their efforts and contributions? Do you value the little things people do for you every day, rather than just waiting for big tasks and projects to be completed? Celebrate others' success before your own. Find reasons to include rather than to exclude. Give other people the "thumbs-up" in your daily experiences. Communicate to people that they have done a good job. Tell people when you value them. When you know someone else is frustrated and discouraged, give them a "thumbs-up" and let them know that you, too, can help.

Perhaps the most important lesson my children have taught me is one about miracles. As adults, we see miracles as events like the parting of the Red Sea. Because we live in an instantaneous world, we get impatient if our progress through life is not filled with one dramatic improvement after another. If we make one significant change in ourselves, we think our next change should be equally significant. One great stride after another, we think. Otherwise, we think, we aren't improving.

But here's what my children taught me: The little changes that take place in the world—a sun setting, a star shooting across the heavens, a small caterpillar growing and turning into a beautiful butterfly, an ugly duckling maturing into a beautiful swan—is just as miraculous as a man standing beside a large body of water, raising his arms in the air, and sending a gigantic body of water parting so that a million people could cross on dry ground.

In fact, there is only one difference between Moses at the Red Sea and a caterpillar transforming into a butterfly. The difference is time.

In your own journey to a better life, you will have dramatic breakthroughs, and then there will be times when you will ask, "How long must I endure this challenge?" What I hope you will remember through the ups and downs of your journey is what I have often called "the power of incrementalism." Rather than "big bang" miracles, some of the greatest miracles you experience in life are received in increments. These can be the little things that you do, such as the attitudes you develop and the goals you set. Small miracles can be the little things you say, the relationships you develop, or the leadership skills you acquire. They can be the small changes you make in your diet and in your exercise, the extra hour you spend at work, or even the extra hour you make sure to spend with your family. These miracles often have to be measured by gains made over days, weeks, months, and often years.

I admit, there were times when I grew weary during my own journey, wondering how long I would have to endure the rigors of just brushing my teeth. But over the years, because of the things I have experienced, I have come to understand the importance of seeing "miracles" the way my children do. A few years after I left the hospital in California, for instance, I went to see a doctor who gave me a complete examination and a battery of tests. He also looked over my previous medical records, which revealed the infamous Dr. Kelly's original diagnosis that I would not be able to live without constant assistance. But here I was, completely independent. Where my arms before had been completely helpless, now I could use them to lift small objects and help me balance. Where my hands had been unproductive, now I could employ them to get the little things I needed. Where before I didn't have the strength to push my wheelchair forward even an inch, now I could play wheelchair sports.

The doctor broke into an amazed smile and announced, "Art, this is amazing. There is no medical explanation for the outstanding progress you've made. This is a miracle."

I smiled at him. "That's exactly what my children would say," I said.

EIGHTEEN

※

Don't Leave Your Valuables Behind

STRATEGY: AS YOU BEGIN MAKING SIGNIFICANT
LIFE CHANGES, MAKE SURE SOME VERY
IMPORTANT THINGS—PRINCIPLES, VALUES, AND
FAITH—NEVER CHANGE

There is no question that life is a series of tradeoffs: If you do something significant in one area of your life, that means you're giving up something else in another area. You do pay a price of some sort. When you see a guy with his $15 million home on beachfront property, your first question might be, "How did he do that?" But your second question should be, "What did he give up for that? What did he sacrifice?" Maybe he had to sacrifice important time with his family and friends. Maybe he sacrificed a healthy social life. Maybe he sacrificed time for himself to maintain hobbies or other interests. Maybe he went so far as to sacrifice his integrity to get that beach house. But make no mistake: he had to have sacrificed something, because nothing is free.

Even though I just spent a previous chapter talking about the impossibility of living a "balanced" life, I don't want your new sense of focus to exclude the very things that make life worth living. You do not have a life worth living if your life consists of doing what it takes to get ahead of the crowd. A successful life is not out-hustling others. It is not working longer hours. It is not being richer than your neighbors. A truly successful life allows you to have structure and spontaneity. It allows you to converge the needs of your work with the needs of yourself and your family. It reminds you that you work to live, not live to work. It keeps you from being consumed by your daily "to do" list. It allows you, even in the midst of your very public occupation, to give yourself private time. And it lets you stop and cherish simple pleasures even on the most hectic and busy of days.

Obviously, there's nothing wrong with being proud of your profession—as long as you know your identity is not tied to what you do. And there's nothing wrong with having great possessions—as long as those possessions are not a factor in determining your sense of self. Ask yourself what would happen to you if you lost the various "props" and "crutches" you previously had been using to help build your self-worth—your job, your nice car and home, your clothes. Could you still be happy? Are you the type who still relies too much on externalized self-esteem—on possessing certain items or associating with certain people or living in the "right" circumstances? Or can you base your self-worth purely on your decision about who you are and what you are capable of doing? Do you nourish those values that make you realize that you are a unique and important person, that you are here on this earth to do something honorable with your life? Do you nourish those philosophical beliefs about what makes us best as individuals—values of honesty, sacrifice, patriotism, family, life, fiscal stewardship, service, selflessness, kindness, chivalry, civic duty, reverence, thriftiness, courage, and conviction? These are the laws of living that provide the best opportunity for happiness, security, love, and contribution. These are the rules we use to govern much of our behavior and human interaction, rules that have been proven by centuries of practice and observation.

In the end, these qualities are the anchors of our souls. They keep us on a steady course despite the high winds and tempestuous waves change creates for us, personally and professionally. They teach us to believe in ourselves, to have the confidence to do what is right even though it may not always be expedient or easy. It is important that each of us rigorously evaluate whether our behavior is congruent with these anchors in our life. Without those anchors, we are prone to do destructive things or allow ourselves to emotionally waste away.

And there is one other great anchor: a belief in a loving, nuturing God. As I have mentioned, I prayed and prayed and prayed in those days after the accident for God to completely heal me and let me walk again. To this day, I continue to pray for God's healing touch on my paralyzed body. Throughout that time and ever since, I have been asked by many people if my belief in God changed because He hasn't healed me the way I asked Him to . . . yet. People have also asked me if I changed my belief in the power of prayer.

"What is the point of praying to God if you are in this condition?" I have been asked. "Why pray to God at all?"

It's a question I put to you. What is the importance of prayer during your own time of crisis or challenge? I want you to know that this is not a chapter designed to convert you to a particular religious practice. I am not here to try to get you to follow the same religious faith that I do. But I am convinced that God works in all of our lives, that He is there to help us lift our lives above the level of mere existence, and that He is always summoning us to be more than we started out to be. One of the world's great psychiatrists, Carl Jung, once wrote that the major problem facing his patients over the age of thirty-five was that they had no religious outlook on life. "It is safe to say that every one of them fell ill because he had lost that which the living religions of every age have given their followers, and none of them has really been healed who did not regain his religious outlook," Jung wrote.

I know the skeptics of the world are wrong when they explain that what happened to me, or anyone in my condition, is a sign that God does not exist—or that God allows horrible things to happen to those who love him. Although I am not a great theologian or philosopher who has all the answers about the way God works—much of God's plan has not been revealed to any of us—I do know that God did not cause my suffering. Tragedy is never God's will. The fact is that bad things just happen every now and then. But the bad things that happen to us do not have a meaning until we give them meaning. We can either lapse into despair by saying God has abandoned us and let us suffer, or we can decide to redeem ourselves from our suffering with God's help. My life is a testament to the power and compassion of God. No matter which direction the circumstances of my life took, He was always there, utterly dependable.

Why pray? Well, first, let me tell you what you're getting—and not getting—if you do pray. A lot of people pray because they think God is some kind of cosmic Santa Claus. I used to believe this. In some ways, my childhood experiences of Christmas—the excitement of waiting for Santa Claus to come down our chimney and bring me presents—became part of my relationship with God. Without meaning to, and without conscious knowledge, I began thinking of God as a Great Being who did nothing but dispense treats to those who have been good and who ask for treats in a very polite voice.

In Sunday School, I was taught the fundamentals of an appropriate prayer: 1. Dear Heavenly Father . . . 2. I thank thee . . . 3. I ask thee. . . . 4. In the name of Jesus Christ, Amen. The emphasis in those prayers always seemed to be on the "I ask thee" part. My prayers were pretty much a "to do" list for God. "Please keep me safe. Watch over me. Help me score well on my test. Keep me out of trouble. Cause my parents to show mercy on me after they find out I wrecked their car. Help Dallas fall in love with me and say yes to my invitation to the prom." And the list went on and on.

Asking for help from God is appropriate, but for a long time, it was 98 percent of my prayers. I raced through the few, trite things I was grateful for in order to make sure I had plenty of time to get my full, prioritized list to the Lord, so that he could work on my demands right away. Unfortunately, such an approach to prayer and faith caused me a lot of discouragement, frustration, and misunderstanding. I had fallen victim to the myth that God's sole duty is to bring me pleasure and grant my wishes.

I also bought into the myth that God would deliver me from the consequences of my bad choices. I told you earlier about the time when I was ten years old and I decided to be G. I. Joe with a parachute, jumping from the top of our two-story house holding a bedsheet. It was about the time I was passing the balcony that I realized I wasn't going to slow down. Suddenly I became a fervent believer in prayer. My lips moved so fast in my attempt to communicate with God that the wind caused them to whistle!

The fall seemed to last an eternity. I made more promises to God during that descent than I could possibly ever have fulfilled. As you can guess, moments later I crashed to the ground at full speed.

At the time, I was disappointed that God had not saved me. Since then, I have had other experiences in which I made inappropriate requests of God in an effort to avoid the natural consequences of my own foolish behavior. I prayed that God would help me score well on a test that was critical to my educational future, yet I never studied for it. I asked my Father in heaven to bless me with good health while I was abusing my body with junk food and poor eating habits. I petitioned him for safety and then drove faster than the posted speed limit without a seat belt on.

As much as God loves his children, it is misplaced faith that asks him to prevent all pain in this life, especially the pain we created for ourselves. When we ask God to remove the natural consequences of our own behavior, we set ourselves up for disappointment and frustration. As a wise friend once said, "It is foolish to think you can sow your wild oats on Saturday and pray for crop failure on Sunday."

There was a third myth about prayer that I bought into. It was that if God did not answer yes to my prayers, it was because I didn't have enough faith. When I heard nothing from God after I asked him to restore me to the health I had enjoyed before the accident left me paralyzed, I would think, "What have I done wrong?"

Because God did not always answer my prayers the way I desired, did it really mean that I was found wanting in His eyes?

No. It meant that I didn't understand God's role in my life and in the life of the world. As a result, I did not understand the true power of God to comfort and to inspire.

I did have the innocent expectation when I was a child that

184 ■ The Impossible Just Takes a Little Longer

good things would always happen to me. I also thought that bad things happened only to bad people. As a teenager, I became embittered as some of the "bad" things in life began coming my way. It just wasn't fair, I thought. The whole eternal plan must be out of whack. Not until years later did I learn that only the innocent and the ignorant expect only good things to happen to them. It takes a greater understanding to comprehend that good can come from all things. The apostle Paul stated the difference perfectly: "All things work together for good to those who love God."

Let's assume God was how we wanted him to be, answering every prayer we sent his way. If God answered yes to all prayers, there would be no sickness, no discomfort, no death, no hunger, no pain, no adversity, no poverty, no challenge, no disappointment. And if there were none of these things, there would be no learning, no growth, and no change. And without growth and change, what would be the point of living? Why live at all if we could not go through the wondrous, mysterious, sometimes painful, but ultimately redeeming journey of life?

It is my testimony that God does love us. But it is not God's purpose to meet our every demand the way we want it met. Rather, He is here to provide support, love, light, and strength. It is my belief that although we sometimes cry out and wish that God would remove all the pain from our lives, He loves us more than that. He loves us enough to bless us with the miracle of time. With the miracle of time, He provides you and me with those very opportunities to grow and to change. He also provides us with the tools to make the changes we need to make. But it is also clear that we have to make those changes ourselves.

There is a passage in the Book of Matthew in which Jesus says, "And all things, whatsoever ye shall ask in prayer, believing, ye shall receive." Most of us don't have any trouble with the asking part. What we have trouble with is the believing part. *Belief* is an action verb. It requires us to do something—to give something back to God. So to ask God to do something for you, you have to be willing to do your part. You have to ask yourself, "Am I willing to do all that is required of me?" Only if you can honestly answer that question "yes" are you ready to petition God for his help.

There is another statement from Jesus: "And that servant, which . . . prepared not himself, neither did according to the [Lord's] will, shall be beaten with many stripes." In other words, if you do not do everything you can to prepare yourself for change, then God isn't going to do it for you. Fear is the opposite of faith. If you want to exercise real faith and eliminate fear, you must be prepared. In fact, one wise person advised that we ought to pray as though everything depended on the Lord and then get up from our knees and work as though everything depended on ourselves.

Are you beginning to see what you must do? Instead of begging God to do something to get you out of this condition, you need to do something yourself. And instead of blaming God for whatever predicament you find yourself in, the better alternative is to express gratitude. It's true. Express gratitude and recognize that whatever tragedy or setback has befallen you can be a way to bring yourself closer to God's love.

In prayer, I now spend twice as much time thanking God for his rich blessings as I do creating my "to do" list for him. Completely aside from the fact that expressing gratitude to God is a commandment, it is also an act of faith. To exercise faith is to act as if our prayers have been answered. If I truly believe that God will hear and answer my righteous desires, I will spend more time thanking rather than just asking.

As we all know, saying prayers of thanks is easy in the midst of abundance. When our lives are going well, when our bills are paid and money is left over, when our children are obedient, it is easy to be grateful. What is hard is being grateful when things aren't going so well. It is hard to praise God while the seas rage. It is hard to be grateful in the midst of pain and struggle. It is hard to thank the Giver of all good things when our plate doesn't seem so full anymore.

Who has time to make prayers of gratitude when pain fills our days?

Does the Lord really expect us to be grateful when things aren't going well? Even though He said we should grateful "in all things," does that mean we should be grateful when we reach the end of our money before the end of the month? Yes. Does that mean we should be grateful when we suffer from loneliness and depression? Yes. Does that mean we should be grateful if our employer terminates us? Absolutely.

Does that seem ridiculous? It might. But there are very valid reasons. It is not that God commands us to be grateful in all things to serve His own selfish purposes, but rather to bless our own lives. Learning to be grateful in all things promotes a measure of peace that we may never know otherwise. In the Old Testament, King David, who certainly had his share of adversity, declared, "I will bless the Lord at all times; his praise shall continually be in my mouth."

Gratitude to God, even in hard times, encourages us to count the source of all blessings. Someone has said that an ungrateful person is like a hog under a tree eating apples and never looking up to see where they come from. When we keep our eyes focused on our problems, we only discover new problems. Years ago, it would have been easy to focus on all the things I could not do— and they were numerous. But by focusing on the things that I could do, I found that God blessed me with more. Before my accident there might have been ten thousand things I could do. Today, I may be able to do only a thousand of them. Nevertheless, I can choose either to focus on the nine thousand things I cannot do, or I can focus on the thousand I still can. By focusing on the one thousand and being grateful for them, I have learned to do so many more.

People still say to me in incredulous tones, "But don't you think what happened to you was wrong? Don't you think it was an act of evil?" I remind them of one of Jesus' statements: "Every good tree bringeth forth good fruit; but a corrupt tree bringeth forth evil fruit. A good tree cannot bring forth evil fruit, neither can a corrupt tree bring forth good fruit . . . Wherefore by their fruits ye shall know them." Because the fruits of my tree (the accident) have been so good—the blessings I have received, the love I have felt, the Spirit that has presided, the relationships that have been built with the Lord and those I love, and the miracles I have experienced—then how can anyone say that the tree is evil? It's all in the way you look at it.

Are you focusing on the problems of your life, or are you considering the blessings God grants you every day? Return the thanks, and God's peace will follow. He knows better than anyone else our wounds and sorrows, the scars on our hearts. And He will be there to help us through our pain. He will be there to inspire us to find the best part of ourselves.

NINETEEN

❋

Be Prepared to Go the Distance

STRATEGY: RECOGNIZE THAT YOUR LIFE
IS NOT A SPRINT, BUT A LONG-DISTANCE JOURNEY

My muscles tensed in the crisp air of the early morning. I adjusted my helmet, secured tape around my wrists and hands, and made final changes to my tucked seating position. An intensity was mounting as the minutes ticked away, but no one spoke. A soft glow was filling the horizon as the sun crept toward the sky. A gun sounded in the clear morning air, and I began the long and arduous race toward St. George, Utah, 325 miles away.

That's right. That's no misprint. It was July 2, 1993, and I was competing in the seven-day, 325-mile-long Salt Lake City to St. George ultra-marathon. I was attempting to race a distance that would be farther than any quadriplegic at my level of ability had ever attempted. One decade after my car wreck, I was going to prove just how far I had come, despite every prediction and diagnosis to the contrary. I was ready to show the naysayers that there was no such thing as a problem too great to handle, and that those problems that do come along will only bring out the best in a person with the right beliefs and the right determination.

Wheelchair racing had long been a passion of mine. It was not something at which I initially did well. Almost all other wheelchair entrants are paraplegics, able to grasp and grip the rings as they push with their back, shoulder, stomach, and tricep muscles working in perfect unison and harmony. As a quadriplegic, I had only the backs of my hands and wrists to propel myself. When I told some of my friends and family that I wanted to compete in wheelchair races, they patted me on the back politely, with plastic smiles on their faces, the way doctors do with crazy people who are beyond help.

But the minute I began talking about wheelchair racing, something started to shift inside me. It was a breakthrough moment. The old me suddenly grew very still inside, and the possible me stirred. Although there was a certain amount of fear that accompanied my proclamation that I would race in a wheelchair, I also felt more animated, more alive. I had shifted my very identity from someone who had a dream to someone who had a tangible goal and plan.

Not that this meant I became an immediate success. At my first race, a five-mile event, I was the last to finish. Runners and wheelchair racers had completed the course and were leaving for home when I came within sight of the finish line. Race organizers were busy taking down the sign marked "FINISH." It had taken two and a half hours to finish the race.

But I resolved to train even harder, and two years later, I completed a ten-kilometer (6.2 mile) race in less than one hour.

Rather than inching my way painfully forward as I had done in the first race, I was steadily pulling away from the runners as the finish line drew nearer and the cheers from the waiting crowd were ringing in my ears.

Then I decided to undergo an even more intense training period in order to race in a regular 26.2-mile marathon. I had read an article about the three-hour barrier in the marathon for wheelchair athletes. The article described this barrier as though it were the Berlin Wall, and it talked about those wheelchair athletes who, after years of training, had, like Roger Bannister of the track world, broken beyond the limits of expectation to set new records below the three-hour mark. On that course of rolling hills, considered to be fairly easy for marathons, I did finish that race, and as I crossed the line, the clock read two hours, fifty-three minutes, and fifty-four seconds. On my first marathon, I had broken through the three-hour wall.

"Hey," I said to my friends and family, "I can do this." Then I told them what I thought should be my next challenge: the Salt Lake to St. George ultra-marathon.

I am sure at least one of my friends tried not to laugh when I told them what I was going to do. And true enough, this was a real stretch. A quadriplegic going up and down the Utah mountains? Besides, I had a problem with not being able to sweat. How was I going to handle the heat, considering that the race was to be run in July?

No problem, I said. I had my family to travel with me as my road crew, their main job being to douse me with ice water over and over to keep my body temperature down.

Three years later, after getting into the best shape anyone in my condition could be, I pulled away from the starting line to begin my seven-day endurance test. The chair I was using was much different from the one I use every day. It weighed only nine pounds and had only three wheels. I raced with my knees tucked into my chest. Since I have no grip with my hands, I used a back-hand pushing technique to maintain speed and momentum. Also, the chair was black. I wore black racing pants, with a black helmet, hot pink tank top, and black sunglasses. Dallas figured that if I wasn't going to win, at least I ought to look good.

By the third day, however, I wasn't looking so good. Although I was averaging nearly fifty miles a day, my hands were so bloody and swollen that my doctor, who had come along to supervise my condition, asked me to consider stopping the race before I did any permanent damage.

I said no. I kept thinking, *It couldn't get any harder than this. Surely it will get better.*

On the fourth day, I faced headwinds of between twenty and thirty miles per hour. The winds were so stiff at times that I had to push even going downhill to keep my speed up. My hands throbbed and ached with every stroke, and I had little opportunity to rest.

But I kept thinking, *It can't get any harder. Surely it will get better.*

On the fifth day, temperatures reached 105 degrees, and I began baking in the heat. My body ached, my muscles felt beyond fatigue, and my breathing was labored at best. For three hours I didn't have the strength to speak to anyone. I put my head down and just kept pushing forward. Each minute I asked myself if I could survive the next minute of pushing. My head became so light that for a time I wasn't sure where I was. With my eyes closed, I focused on the sounds and patterns of my breathing to give me a rhythm to hold onto. Then, after several minutes, I realized the sounds of my breathing had become mixed with the sounds of someone walking briskly next to me. Assuming that a member of my family had joined me as a source of support, I kept my eyes closed. More minutes passed. There was still someone right there, walking and breathing beside me. With each push, I gained a greater sense of calm, and finally I had the strength to open my eyes to thank whoever it was for being there.

The horizon stretched beside me, empty. There was no one around. No one was next to me at all. I looked over my shoulder. The nearest person to me was my sister Beverly, on a bike some thirty yards behind me. I kept looking around, and I realized that the sound of footsteps had stopped as abruptly as they had come.

Had I experienced an illusion? Had I made the whole thing up in my heat-stroked brain? I was never able to say for sure. But whoever had come to walk that hot and difficult road with me had left me inspired to get through that day.

Still, there were two days left, and the sixth day was the most difficult. With temperatures still breaking 100 degrees, I came to the base of a mountain that seemed to go up forever. As the road got steeper, my pace got slower. The angle of the chair was at such a sharp incline that I had to keep my head lowered toward my knees. If I raised my head just a little, the front wheels rose off the surface of the road. A steep ascent was what prominently displayed the difference between quadriplegic and paraplegic racers. Without hand strength to grip the ring, and no right tricep to endure the climb, I slowed to a crawl.

At one point, as I pressed against the push ring, my glove slipped, and my chair immediately began to roll backward. I reached quickly for the brake on the front wheel. With none of my body weight over my front wheel, however, my wheelchair skidded across the road as I rolled backward. I knew if I grabbed for my push rings, I would flip over backward. Suddenly, before I tumbled into a deep ravine, my sister Beverly grabbed my chair, stopping a sure disaster.

When I was back on the road, going forward, I knew I was facing an uncomfortable decision. All the warning signs had begun to go off. My muscles strained and ached, and my shoulders had begun to feel numb. The tape from my wrists had worn down, and my gloves were slipping from my hands. Because the sun continued to beat down relentlessly, my body temperature began to rise. I looked up the road and watched as it continued its steep climb, curving out of sight. Glancing up the road, careful to keep my chin to my knee, I thought to myself, "I will push just one hundred more times, and then I will quit. I mean, who would blame me? This is the farthest I have ever gone." Slowly, methodically, I began the long count, "One, two, three . . ."

After reaching 100, I looked again at the continuing climb and thought, "I'll push just one hundred more times, and then I'll stop. The relief vehicles can take me to the finish line and I will still have won a great battle. Who would expect me to finish anyway? One . . . two . . . three . . ."

I inched my way up the road. If someone had told me then that the climb would continue for several miles, I probably would have quit right there. Every struggle, every moment of suffering, every outcry by me for help had been met with words of encouragement whispered by the spirit, "Come on, Art! Don't give up, Art. You can make it, Art. Come on, Art." It was the central message of my story and every story of human suffering and sacrifice. The effect was so profound as to leave my cheeks wet with tears. On that mountain, thinking about those words, my strength became renewed, and reaching into depths of ability and endurance I had not previously possessed, I moved the chair forward.

I inched my way up that mountain for thirteen hours, gloves slipping, blisters forming, and muscles always on the verge of collapse. The road climbed twelve miles to nearly 9,000 feet. Thousands of pushes later, I was, amazingly, at the top. And there, I learned one very valuable truth: with every up, there is a down, and sometimes those downs can be a blessing. I started flying down the other side of the mountain, my wheelchair hitting speeds of nearly 40 miles per hour. The last fifty miles passed quickly. I could smell the finish line. Seven days after I left Salt Lake City, I rolled the final miles into St. George. I had set a world record, becoming the first quadriplegic of my classification to complete an ultra-marathon in seven days. On my final push to the finish line in the heart of town, police stopped traffic, and people lined the streets as I raced by. Tears fell from my eyes. I had made it. Then I knew that what my mother had said was true: "While the difficult takes time, the impossible just takes a little longer."

Why did I do it? Why did I put myself through such extreme effort? Why did I want to do something that made my lungs burn and my body ache, something that gave me a pounding headache and made me feel nauseated from all the physical stress?

Of course, I didn't have to enter that race. No one made me do it. I could have taken it easy. It wasn't as if I didn't have enough things to work on already.

But something inside me kept saying, "I need to compete. I need to push my body and mind. I can't stop here in my life. I need to go the distance." I didn't enter the ultra-marathon to set a record or to get attention or to receive some flattering headlines in the newspapers. On one level, I did the race to improve my life as a quadriplegic. I knew that by setting such a difficult task in front of myself, racing 325 miles over seven days, I would be required to train in such a way as I never had before. If I could increase my strength and endurance by just ten percent, it would give me thousands of more things I could do. At another level, I knew the ultra-marathon would teach me to be sharper mentally. It would increase my mental strength, my ability to concentrate and to endure and to stay disciplined. I was just fine where I was—after all, I had already completed a normal marathon in under three hours, which few other athletes at my level of ability had ever before done—but I wanted to keep pressing, to keep expanding my boundaries, to push myself out of my comfort zone.

And that is precisely the attitude we must all have when it comes to the way we live our lives. The comfort zones you have created—due to your fears of failure, your fears that you are not good enough—are very powerful forces. Most of you have spent your life in your comfort zones. To use an automobile analogy, you adamantly have stayed in the far right lane on a highway, refusing to get up to even the minimum speed limit. You've formed a lot of self-protective decisions and beliefs that reinforce the fact that we shouldn't do this or that. The longer you've been in that zone, the more you have lost your courage, restricted your world, and skewed your behavior in order to avoid situations that might threaten your safety.

Getting out of your comfort zone is not easy. It can't be done in one short sprint to the finish. It takes a long time. To live a self-designed life—to secure real happiness and personal satisfaction—you need the tenacity and determination of someone running an ultra-marathon. In my training for that 325-mile race across Utah, there were certain characteristics I had to develop. To reach a significant destination in your life, you must develop the same characteristics. There are five major lessons in the ultra-marathon of your own life:

1. Self-Motivation

In life, you have to be self-motivated. No one is going to force you to improve your lot in life. No "coach" is going to give you the per-

fect rah-rah speech that will drive you to victory. No special bene-
factor is going to arrive and provide you with the perfect circumstances that will give you the incentive to achieve. You must create
your own circumstances that will motivate you, and you alone, to
act. The foundation for motivation is emotion—great achievers in
any endeavor seem to possess passion and emotion.

2. Preparation

An ultra-marathon places physical, mental, and emotional demands
on an athlete. When the starting gun fires, the competitor had
better be prepared. A new life outside your comfort zone is also
going to place certain new demands on you—physical, mental,
emotional, and sometimes financial. If you know the demands
you're facing, then they won't come as a surprise. Two Harvard
psychologists did a study of people who considered themselves
happy. They found that what these people had in common was
not money or good health or a loving romantic relationship.
What they had in common was that they knew what they
wanted and they felt they were moving in the right direction to
get it. That's what made life feel great. They were headed for
something they knew would make them, in the end, feel far more
valuable.

3. Pace

Setting the right pace is critical in a long-distance race. There's no
point in starting out full speed ahead, leaving all opponents at the
starting line, only to collapse from exhaustion a couple of miles
into the race. Pacing is absolutely essential for you, too, as you
travel down your new road in life. If you're in too much of a hurry,

you'll inevitably hit potholes you didn't see, or find yourself on a detour you didn't expect.

4. Focus

One particular day during my preparation, my training was going well. I felt strong and aggressive. My speeds were increasing and my strokes were becoming more fluid. Wheeling along at about fifteen miles per hour, I came quickly around a bend. Some activity on the road ahead temporarily distracted my attention from the road surface in front of me. Before I knew it, my racing wheelchair had slammed into a curb, flown in the air, and turned sideways. Still in my chair, I came crashing to the ground and slid for several yards across the asphalt road. Only my helmet saved me from a head injury. My arms and elbows were raw and bloody. Bystanders ran to lift me and my chair back to the proper position. It would have been easy to become discouraged about my injuries and stop my training at that moment. But I kept reminding myself—and reminding myself, and reminding myself—that I was training for something that would far outweigh the pain.

I will be the first to tell you, there are going to be moments when you can't even imagine lifting your head to get a look at the prize. There were so many times during the ultra-marathon when the heat or physical exhaustion were so overwhelming that I literally didn't have the strength to look up and see the horizon before me. I didn't even want to think about how far I had to go, because it was too overwhelming. As a result, there were hours at a time when I simply looked at the white lines on the highway that passed directly underneath my feet. All I could do, all I could emotionally and physically manage, was what was right in front of me.

When you reach that grueling point in your own life journey, don't panic and think about giving up. In reality, there will be times when you are so overwhelmed yourself that you won't even be able to imagine that there is a finish line. You won't have time for dreamy ideas. You won't smile much. At that point, you must lower your head and plow forward. The path to our deepest dreams and desires is not an endeavor for on-again, off-again athletes. It's a feat of stamina, a sunup-to-sunset trek toward that horizon. Just as an ultra-marathoner must appreciate the total effort, from conception to completion, you, too, must appreciate the intense pain that inevitably will be a part of your effort. To avoid the pain that comes with struggle is to eliminate the chance for true improvement. You forfeit the opportunity to discover who you can be. To be alive is to feel pain—and once you know that, then you are better able to handle the hard times with a sense of pride and, above all, a sense of accomplishment and self-worth.

5. *Momentum*

There is one last lesson that comes from an ultra-marathon. At some point, when you break through the pain, when you get to that top of that difficult twelve-mile mountain climb, you begin to take off. You can capture the power of momentum, and then you become virtually unstoppable. In your own life journey, you are going to feel extremely anxious and ill at ease as you break out of your comfort zone and find yourself in new, imposing, fearful territory. Your stomach might feel squeamish and your head dizzy. Your anxiety may express itself physically in a loud and piercing voice that will advise you, "This may be dangerous." You will look back and wonder if you should just head back down the mountain to the safe, comfortable, boring valley below, even though you know it's that valley where you lived with anxiety, despair, and fear. But if you keep looking up, if you just keep going a little bit further, one day at a time, you'll start finding your momentum. And soon you'll be bursting through life at full speed.

PART FOUR

The Joy of
the Journey

TWENTY

Continuing the Journey
Toward a Life of Meaning

There is no question that my life has been dramatically changed in many ways because of my accident years ago. What a contrast my life has been since those early days. When I lay in that bed with a broken neck, I wondered if all my hopes, dreams, and ambitions had been broken with it. My new future was carefully explained to me in painful detail. None of the plans included working, driving a vehicle, getting married and enjoying a fulfilling relationship, being independent, or participating in the sports I loved. I may not be what I should be, or I may not be what I could be, but thank God that I am not what I used to be.

A few years ago, I decided to go back for a visit to the Santa Clara hospital where I had spent so much time and try my luck again at the indoor one-eighth-mile track which I had struggled over in an effort to get a manual wheelchair. I had finished it that first time in twenty-eight minutes. This time, there was no one there except me—no doctors, nurses, therapists, or even Dallas to encourage me. The tape was still on the floor, cracked and yellowing. Using the second hand on my watch to time myself, I took off. Exactly one minute and fifty-eight seconds later, I crossed that line again! I reflected back over the months and years of effort, prayers, faith, and struggle that had brought me to this simple point in time and experience. I could not have felt happier. To other people, it might have been just an interesting accomplishment, but to me, it was another one of those "small" miracles that meant everything.

Since that day I now own and operate two companies. One is my professional speaking company. The other is a dot-com start-up company, and I tell people that as soon as I have lost enough money, I am going to go public! I'm a published author and a professional speaker. Because I am able to drive and get around through airports, I go where I want to go and I do what I want to do. It took me four years to learn how to put my pants on again and five years to learn how to put my shoes and socks on again, but now I am completely independent and able to take care of myself. After being able to type about one word a minute, I persisted in practicing my typing, and if you were to watch me today, you would see me typing at speeds of forty words per minute and better, using only two fingers.

My wife, Dallas, and my two children have been such blessings in my life. In 1992, Dallas was named Mrs. Utah and she was third runner-up to Mrs. USA. That same year, I was named the Young Entrepreneur of the Year for a six-state region by the Small Business Administration, and in 1994, *Success* magazine honored me as one of the Great Comebacks of the Year. Upon joining the prestigious National Speakers Association, I set my sights firmly on earning its highest accreditation, that of Certified Speaking Professional (CSP). It was a process that would require diligent effort, quality control, and measurable results—the benchmark of excellence and quality for the craft and art of professional speaking. Among other things, I would be required to maintain meticulous records of speaking engagements and my interactions with the clients. I had to provide a minimum number of presentations to a minimum number of clients over a specific period of time. I needed educational credits to demonstrate that I was continually learning and growing as a professional speaker and businessman. I was required to demonstrate that I understood and applied the eight core competencies of our trade. Finally, dozens of my clients would be randomly queried to test my application of the skills required to carry the distinction of "CSP" after my name. Five years from the day I joined NSA, I qualified for the CSP designation—the minimum period of time required to be considered.

On February 14th, 2000, while in a hotel room in Orlando, Florida, I received a phone call that reduced me to tears and an overwhelming sense of humility. I had been selected for induction into the National Speakers Association CPAE Speaker Hall of Fame. CPAE stands for Council of Peers Award of Excellence. Since 1977, this award had been given to some of the most elite speakers in the country, including Zig Ziglar, Denis Waitley, Les Brown, Nido Qubein, and others. Its honorary members included President Ronald Reagan and General Colin Powell. To become a member of the CPAE Speaker Hall of Fame wasn't something you could objectively earn. It wasn't something for which you could politic or lobby for. Your peers nominated you, and a rigorous selection process narrowed the choices to only five a year. It is like a lifetime achievement award for speaking, excellence, and professionalism. The award is not based on celebrity status, number of speeches, amount of income, or volunteer involvement in the

National Speakers Association. Inductees are evaluated by their peers through a rigorous and demanding process. Each candidate must excel in seven categories: material, style, experience, delivery, image, professionalism, and communication.

On August 9, 2000, in a ballroom filled with 2,000 people in Washington, D.C., I was presented the award with my family and parents by my side. Choking back emotion from the stage, I thanked my peers and accepted the award and honor. One of the ideas that moved me the most was an experience I had had with my son only weeks earlier. While driving Dalton to school one morning I asked him, "What would you like to be when you grow up?"

He answered, "I would like to be a parent."

"That's great," I responded. "But what do you want to do for a living—to make money?"

His answer came just as quickly. "I want to be a speaker."

This one shocked me because I had never heard him refer to anything like this before. My curiosity was really piqued. "Why do you want to be a speaker?" I asked, trying to dig deeper.

"So that I can talk about my kids," he said. My son, I realized, understood. It wasn't a wish for honor, fame, or glory that made me a speaker. It wasn't overwhelmingly important that my peers recognized and respected me. What was important was that my children loved me and were proud of me. What more can we do in life that is greater than to meet the simple and high expectations of our children? Since starting our family, I have found a deeper and lasting source of personal and professional motivation. I want to be a hero to my children. A few weeks after my Hall of Fame induction, while McKenzie was in fourth grade, I promised her that I would come to her school that afternoon (as I often do). As the day dragged on, small details at the office kept pushing the time for me to go to her school further and further back. I finally realized that if I didn't leave at that moment, school would be out. I dropped what I was doing and left. As I slipped quietly into the back of McKenzie's classroom, I saw her glance over her shoulder and see me. Her eyes lit up and a smile spread across her face. In a whisper, I heard her tell a friend sitting next to her, "I knew he'd come."

It's hard to imagine feeling happier than at the moment. In fact, I have often been asked how happy I would be if there was a medical miracle and I could get the chance to walk again. Since Christopher Reeve's accident, public awareness about spinal cord injuries and research related to it have been high. A lot of money has been raised to support cutting-edge research. I have spoken personally with neuroscientists at University of California at Irvine. The question has not been if they'll find a cure, but when. When I broke my neck in 1983, I knew then that one day I would walk again, and I still believe that today as firmly as I did then.

However, on the day that I do walk, I will be no happier than I am today. I discovered a long time ago that my happiness is not a condition of my circumstances. Rather, happiness is a choice, and I make it every day. While we cannot control the environment of change that is happening all around us, we can control how we respond to it. We can adapt. We can change. And we can still find happiness, no matter how dark the storms are around us.

Of course, my journey is far from over. And so is yours. Our journey is never complete. The struggles never end. The ordeals never stop. Your future will contain more pain and tragedy, more disappointment and frustration, more despair and heartache. You will find yourself working so hard at times that you will feel as Winston Churchill did when he declared, "I have nothing to offer but blood, toil, tears and sweat." You will realize, time and again, that life always brings thorns, problems, and pain.

But remember this very important point: the well-lived life is never a destination, but a process. The joy of this adventure is not in finishing it, but in undertaking the journey itself. The joy is in learning how to call forth your courage and your wisdom in times of need. It is in teaching yourself how to grow mentally and spiritually, not in spite of life's tough times, but because of them. It is in finding your essence out of the hurt and betrayal you have endured.

The longer you continue the journey, the more exciting it becomes, because of the chance you have to learn about who you really are and what you can do. Not only do you get to live and learn, you get to learn and live. As the journey continues, you will find increased personal freedom because you will know how to beat back more of your fears. You will find a greater sense of peace because you will no longer be as paralyzed by life's darker moments. And you will be able to relish whatever it is you are experiencing right now because you will no longer be worrying so deeply about will happen tomorrow. Think of your life as a good book. The further you get into it, the more it begins to come together and make sense. There is meaning in the incidents that you experience. With each new chapter, each new twist of the plot, your character becomes more fully developed. And in the end, there is a satisfying sense of completeness to the character and the story.

By now, I do hope you realize that adversity does not need to lead us away from our best ambitions, but closer to them. You only have to work, struggle, believe, and climb. Just think for a moment about the most optimistic, emotionally healthy, and vibrant people you know. The ones I know who operate at their highest capabilities are people who simply don't fear whatever life throws at them. Their attitude of non-fearful living has led to an almost massive upheaval in their everyday actions, transforming them from people who once thought they "should" or "ought to" find a better life into people who believe they "must" find a better life. Because they know they can handle anything that comes their way, they live with an insatiable hunger to rise up regardless of the circumstances they face, shed the cocoon of limitations, surpass all reasonable expectations, and focus with a fierce, laser beam–like intensity on those dreams that they most want to achieve. They are so determined that they are never going to settle for anything less than something remarkable. They are never going to leave themselves short.

That, too, is the way you are about to live. Rather than being driven by anxieties that cause you to act selfishly and self-destructively, you will be driven to act more honestly, more compassionately, and more nobly. Rather than fearing failure, you will be finding yourself more willing to fail because you know you will get right up and try again. And instead of worrying about the shadow of death, you will be living in such a way that you find yourself consumed by the joy and satisfaction of life in the present.

What's more, when the end of your days on this earth arrives, you will know that you did not waste your life with nothing to show for it. You will also have the great sense of satisfaction that you were responsible for your life, that you were responsible for the way it turned out. You will know that you went through this world not saying, "What does life have in store for me?" but instead asking, "What am I doing with my life?" Even if projects and new ventures do not work out, even if you undergo more disappointment or more suffering, at least you had the fulfilling experience of putting yourself into your life 100 percent.

And you learned that no matter what kind of pain was thrown

your way, you were able to endure it. Rather than running from pain, rather than spending your time asking why pain had to happen or figuring out who to blame for your pain, rather than fearing pain, you gritted your teeth and let the pain hurt—and you eventually outlasted it. Instead of adversity being the obstacle that kept you from completeness, instead of it being the obstacle on the road to your happiness and fulfillment, instead of it causing you to detour away from your hopes, dreams, and most righteous aspirations, it was actually the thing that headed you right toward them.

Some years ago, I went to an amusement park with my family and some friends. My brother Paul, who was with us, helped lift me into the seat of each ride. We rode the roller coaster, the train, the water rides, and every other ride that looked entertaining. At the end of the day, we waited in line for the bumper cars.

Helping me into a bumper car, I had Paul leave me alone in my car while he got another one for himself. Using my arms, I lifted my leg and placed my foot directly over the accelerator pedal. Pushing down with my hand on my knee, I could control the forward movement of the bumper car. As the bell sounded and all the cars lurched forward, I pushed down on my knee and off I went. I steered with one hand and pushed down on my knee with the other.

At first I tried to avoid getting hit by other cars. Soon, however, I was right in the heart of it, bumping head to head with everyone else. Every time I got hit, my foot would leave the accelerator and my leg would fly into the air. Regaining my balance, and trying to brace against other collisions, I would position my foot on the pedal and off I would go, seeking revenge. Suddenly I'd get hit again from the side, and off my foot would fly. I couldn't stop laughing as I tried to get repositioned again.

Those who knew what I was doing tried to keep me from my task, and so while I was trying desperately to reposition myself, they'd ram my car from the side, sending me falling over in my seat, laughing all the while. They laughed, too. They should have—it was me who looked ridiculous! The final buzzer sounded the end of our ride, and it was time to go. Of all the rides that day, the bumper cars brought me the most pleasure and enjoyment.

Life is in many ways the same as that ride. At first we may try to avoid every collision, every mishap. Soon, however, we realize that protection nullifies the purpose of the ride itself. Sure, the bumps are often hard, and when we are first hit, it makes our heads spin. But recovering from the bumps, somehow we feel more alive. We laugh, reposition ourselves, build our faith and strength, brace ourselves, and then get rammed again from the side. When all is said and done, the ride of life is one of great pleasure, hard times and all. To avoid the bumps is to deny growth, happiness, and life's purpose.

Do you remember the request I made of you at the very beginning of this book? I wanted you to ask yourself a couple of questions as you read about my life. Did I really endure a tragedy, or was I given one of the most significant opportunities of my life? Did my life turn into a disaster, or had I been given one of the most significant blessings that I will ever enjoy?

Now that you are the end of the book, what is your answer?

I'll tell you my answer to those questions by telling you one last story. It is a story that you probably would not have understood a couple of hundred pages ago. But I think you will now.

Recently I was going to fly from Salt Lake City to Idaho Falls, Idaho, to give a speech. It was a Boeing 737 holding about 120 passengers, and the flight was scheduled to make a stop in Jackson Hole, Wyoming, on the way to Idaho Falls. As the plane began to descend toward Jackson Hole, however, the pilot's voice came over the intercom and said, "We're having some trouble with our landing gear." I was no expert in aviation, but I was fairly certain the landing gear was a really important part of the plane. The pilot added that the landing gear was down on the wings, but that they were having trouble getting the landing gear down on the nose. "We're not going to stop in Jackson Hole, but we're going to continue on to Idaho Falls," he said. "That will give us more time to work out some of the trouble."

A few minutes later we started to descend toward Idaho Falls. The pilot's voice came back again and said, "Listen, we're still having some trouble with that landing gear. We've tried it electrically, we've tried it manually, we just have no indication that it's down and even if it is down, we're certain it's not locked into position. So for that reason, we're not going to land in Idaho Falls. We're going to return to Salt Lake City. This will give us the opportunity to consume the majority of our fuel." He said they have longer runways and better emergency crews in Salt Lake City to handle this kind of a landing. Now there's a confidence-builder!

As we were returning to Salt Lake City, the flight attendant started to go through some instructions on how to prepare for our circumstances. She instructed those who were wearing glasses to remove them. She instructed those who had pens or pencils in their pockets to take them out. Now there's an interesting observation: We're getting ready to crash our plane and she's worried about me poking myself with my pencil! She asked us to check the security of our seatbelts and instructed us on how to brace ourselves for the initial impact. After some instruction, the flight attendant came to my seat and she said, "Mr. Berg, do you have any questions"? I said that I had only two questions. The first one was, "Am I getting all my frequent flier miles for this? Because we're flying all the way up there and all the way back, which should be double miles." She agreed, even though she was a little startled that I was trying to be funny in such a situation. My second question, though, was of a much more serious nature: "Are these miles transferable?" She didn't find that real funny, either.

As we were approaching Salt Lake City, the pilot said that we would fly in front of the tower at about 180 miles an hour and about 500 feet off the ground so those in the tower could do a visual on our front landing gear. As we flew by the tower, we were so close that we could actually see some of the individuals inside. Down below passengers were lined up in front of the terminal windows to observe what was happening. Out the other side of the aircraft, I could see the runway being lined with fire trucks, emergency crews, and ambulances. And they were starting to spray a foam out on the runway to reduce some of the friction on impact.

As I looked back over my shoulder, I noticed that some of the passengers just stared blankly forward. Others nervously talked to someone who was sitting next to them. Some of them had tears in their eyes or rolling down their cheeks. Others were on the phone. One guy, I think, was selling his stock in the airline we were on. (I am pretty sure that they call that "insider trading.")

This was literally the kind of time when your life does flash in front of your eyes—a time when you think back on everything that has happened to you, everything you've done, and everything you wished you had done. It was also an opportunity to reflect on those you loved. As we made our final approach back toward that runway, the pilot said he would keep the nose of the plane off the ground as long as he could. But in all likelihood, when the nose gear touched ground it would collapse under the weight of the plane, and we'd drop down onto the belly and slide across the runway at more that 130 miles an hour. So he instructed us to brace ourselves.

During those last few minutes, I wondered, "If I had to do it all over again, what would I change? What would I do differently?" I asked myself again a question that a friend had once asked me. "Art," he said, "if you could go back in time to change that Christmas Day in 1983, would you? If you could go back and have yourself fly in a plane from California to Utah, drive with a different friend, or travel during the day to have avoided all the pain you have suffered in your life, would you?"

As the plane continued to circle, I thought about those questions. I thought about the enormous changes I had experienced, the suffering I had endured. And I thought about the meaning I had found on the other side of those experiences. I thought about how that accident so long ago had led me to live clearly and courageously, to see the miraculous in ordinary things, to love others in ways that I never before knew were possible, and to feel the kind of love in return, from others and from God, that was beyond description.

The plane headed toward the runway. The rear wheels touched. We all waited silently as the nose gear lowered toward the ground. We heard the rubber screech on the asphalt below, and the nose gear held. We were brought to a safe stop on the runway and eventually towed toward the terminal.

"No," I said on the airplane that day. "I wouldn't change a thing about my life. I wouldn't go back and change the day of that accident. I thank God that life was hard. And I thank God that life is still hard today."

And so my journey continues. Your journey continues. My prayer is that you will find the rich blessings that I have found. They are right there before you. All you have to do is take a step forward.

Live each day with purpose and passion. The impossible just takes a little longer.

Do the impossible.

POSTSCRIPT

A rt Berg passed away—suddenly, tragically—on February 19, 2002, just weeks before the publication of *The Impossible Just Takes a Little Longer*. Sadly, he had not yet even seen a copy of the finished book. His survivors included his wife, Dallas, and their three young children, McKenzie, Dalton, and Peyton.

On February 11, 2003, nearly a year after its publication, *The Impossible Just Takes a Little Longer* was given the Books for a Better Life Award for best motivational book of 2002. Although Dallas and the children were unable to make the trip to New York for the awards presentation, McKenzie Berg sent the following remarks to be read at the ceremony:

I am so proud to accept this award for my father. If he were here to do this himself, he would push his wheelchair to the microphone, smile that wonderful smile, and say something funny—not a joke, but something funny—probably about himself.

Then he'd build a bridge to you with his words. It might be something about pain, so you'd all listen and understand, because he knew we all have pain.

Or maybe he'd say something to remind you that miracles do happen, even if sometimes the miracles take time.

Or his bridge of words might stir a thought or idea—hiding somewhere inside behind a frustration or fear—to dare to do the impossible.

Whatever the words, something like hope and dreams and daring all mixed up together would wash over you and you'd never forget his name—Art Berg—or the way you felt inside when he talked to you. Because my dad touched people with his words, and changed their lives forever.

I'm so proud of my dad. Thank you for being proud of him, too.

I'm McKenzie Berg—and I'm twelve years old today.

William Morrow, Quill, and HarperCollins are proud to have been associated with *The Impossible Just Takes a Little Longer*. Art's courage, determination, and great heart were a lasting gift to all who knew him. As McKenzie says, he built bridges with words, and those bridges live on in his book.